DRIVE YOUR ADVENTURE

Original publisher: © Editions Apogée, 2020
© English publication: Lannoo Publishers, Tielt, 2021
ISBN 978 94 014 6703 2
D/2021/45/89 – NUR400/510
www.lannoopublishers.com

Translation: Clare & Mike Wilkinson, Tessera Translations, Wageningen
Lay-out: Asterisk*, Amsterdam

If you have any questions or comments about the material in this book, please do not hesitate to contact our editorial team: redactiekunst@lannoo.com

DRIVE YOUR ADVENTURE

Portugal

Clémence Polge and Thomas Corbet

Lannoo

Foreword

In 2017, Clémence (an architect and designer) and I, Thomas (a journalist and translator), became genuine 'nomads 2.0' when we decided to travel around Europe full-time and work on the road. Our route was due to take us from the south northwards to Scandinavia but we got interrupted in Denmark by a great opportunity. In 2018, we were chosen by WeVan to take the wheel in Lagertha, the camper van that let us explore and rediscover Norway on a two-month adventure. That was a summer trip that kept us going until the next spring, when our account of our travels – Drive Your Adventure: Norway by Camper Van (the French edition) – was published as the second book in the DYA series.
Then without warning, the project team asked us a question we really hadn't been expecting: "Would you guys be interested in a new trip this year?" After taking time to consider the matter – a good ten seconds – well, you can guess our answer, and that was the next destination sorted.
This time, the journey would be a completely new experience for both of us. An experience that we are very happy to share with you in the following pages. Climb on board and we'll take you to Portugal!

Clémence Polge and Thomas Corbet

2019 EDITION
DRIVE YOUR
ADVENTURE

Contents

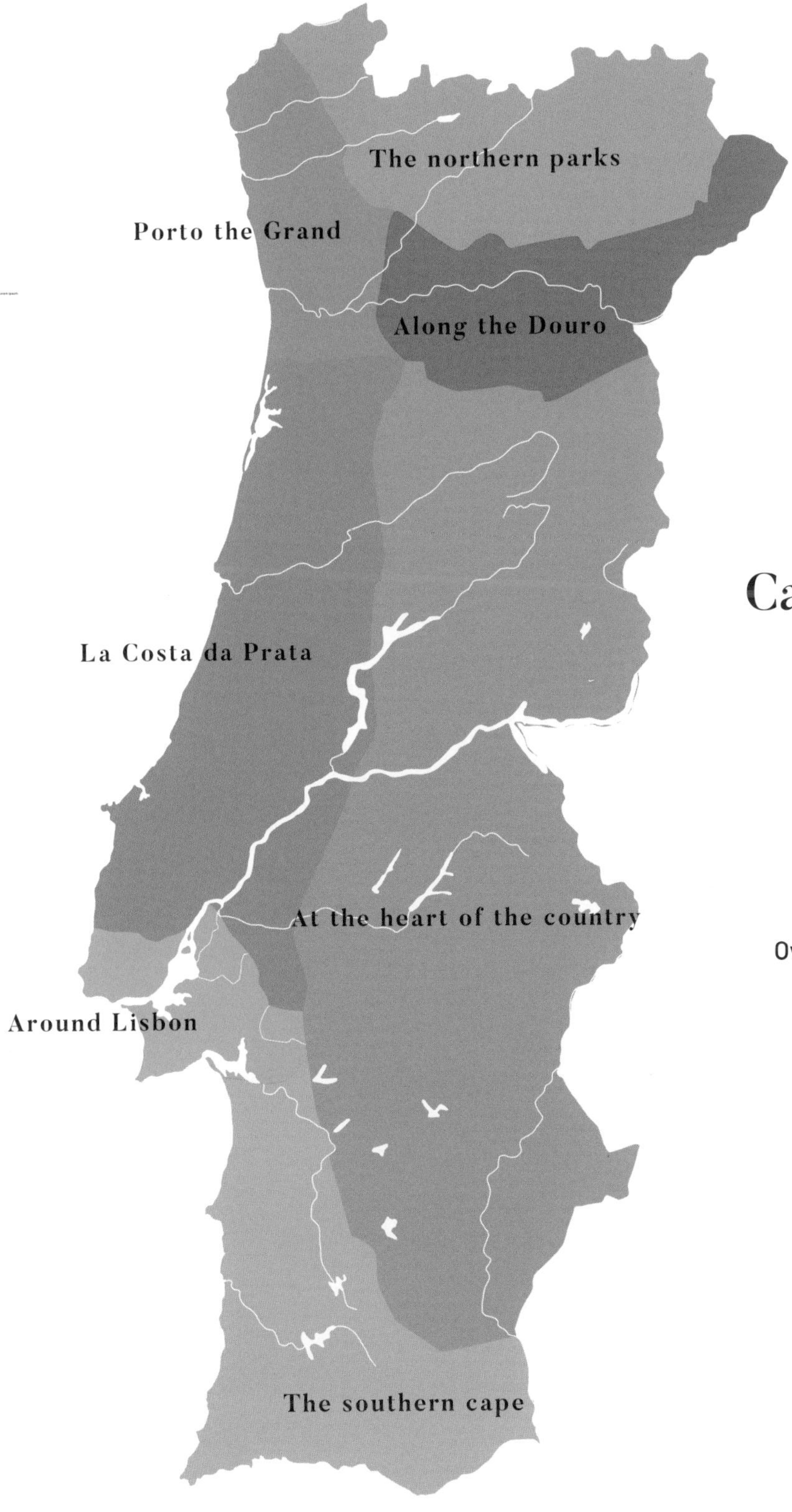

Categories

Stop-overs

Overnight spots

Activities

Meet-ups

Recipes

Preparing your Portugal trip properly

The major Portuguese regions

Like its European neighbours, Portugal can look back on a long history marked by numerous conflicts, periods when it was ruled by foreign powers, independence from the kingdom of León in 1143 and referendums with varying degrees of success. Which explains why the administrative organization of Portugal's territory can look rather chaotic to an uninitiated observer. Continental Portugal is divided into five regions (there are also two autonomous island regions, the Azores and Madeira). But it's also divided into eighteen districts and the district borders aren't even always aligned with the regional borders. So some districts straddle two regions... Are you keeping up?

If not, relax: the five continental regions are a purely theoretical entity because the referendum in 1998 that was supposed to ratify them was declared a failure. Despite this, the regions still give the best representation of the country's geographical divisions.

So here they are, from north to south:
Norte: the country's northern section, with Porto as its capital
Centro: bordered on the north by Norte, this region stretches as far as Lisbon. Its capital is Coimbra

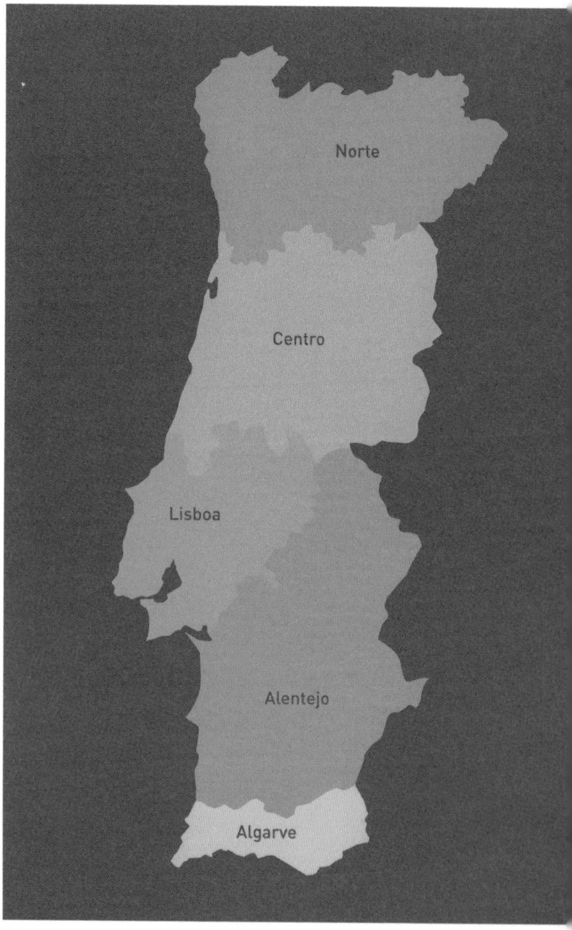

Lisboa: the region around Lisbon
Alentejo: the largest region, its capital is Évora
Algarve: the far south of the country, including the district of its capital, Faro

To let us stick as closely as possible to our perceived experience and to balance the various parts of our narrative, we decided to divide our journey into seven zones, which we'll let you discover as you turn these pages!
One geographical point to remember: don't forget Portugal is one hour behind Scandinavia and most of continental Europe (France, Germany, the Benelux and so on – the same as the UK and Ireland).

Climate

No matter where you are in Portugal, your legs will never be long enough for you to dip so much as a toe in the Mediterranean. Despite that, the country still has a Mediterranean climate, with certain caveats.

The climate in the southern half of Portugal is essentially Mediterranean, characterized by hot, dry summers and relatively mild winters where the temperature virtually never drops below zero. This is not quite so true for the northern half, where summers are not as hot and, in particular, they have more rain all year long. In fact, certain zones in the north and various mountain chains can even experience periods of ice and snow in the winter.

The coastal climate is affected by the Atlantic Ocean, with fewer temperature extremes than further inland.

With its hot summers, when you can nevertheless easily find somewhere to cool down, and its mild winters, Portugal could actually be considered the ideal destination for camper van travellers, from January to December!

The administrative formalities

Portugal became a member of the European Economic Community (EEC) in 1986 and then the European Union, so there's no problem for European citizens, who can come and go as they please. You don't need a visa if you have a valid identity card or European passport.

One relevant piece of information for drivers in particular is that EU driving licences are valid in Portugal. All you have to do is check that your van's insurance covers Portugal (plus all the countries you're travelling through), given that foreign number plates often get targeted by thieves and other marauders of the highways. If you take valuables with you, remember to include them in your cover or insure them against theft. (UK nationals will have to check all these various aspects, as the details are in a state of flux and not known at the time this book went to press.)

Health

You may not necessarily want to think about it when planning your trip, but it's always better to be prepared for any eventuality. All the more so when it comes to health.

There are two solutions available to travellers:
• A European Health Insurance Card (which you can get through your usual channels) to cover your health expenses and get access to care without having to make advance payments, in the same way as Portuguese who are insured.
• Retrospective reimbursement through your usual health insurance company.
Before you leave, make sure you can benefit from repatriation insurance through your credit card or mutual insurance company. And check whether specific high-risk activities are excluded (diving, surfing and sometimes even hiking).

As far as vaccinations are concerned, no specific vaccines are recommended for trips to Portugal (from France at any rate). Just make sure you are up to date with the standard vaccines. And that is good advice even if you won't be doing more than leaf through this guide...

While we're on the subject, don't forget to vaccinate your furry friend if necessary (rabies vaccine). And if said friend is more scaly or feathery than furry, perhaps you would be better off asking a neighbour to feed it while you're away?
Our tip: there are sites that list tips and formalities for preparing your trip, broken down by animal and by country. (Again, UK nationals and residents will need to check the details.)

Travellers going in the summer should watch out for sunstroke, especially in the south and

on the coast where the sun can get pretty strong in the afternoon. Stay hydrated!
Finally, you wouldn't be properly prepared for your camper van trip if you didn't have this guide on the one hand, and on the other if you don't have a decent first aid kit containing some medicines, bandages, disinfectant, creams for abrasions and sunburn, and so on.

Connectivity

For those who will be leaving with all their multimedia equipment, Portuguese sockets are standard European ones (so British and Irish travellers will need an adapter for their type G plugs). So most Europeans won't need to set off with a host of different adapters for charging their computers, phones etcetera. A cool tip: if you're going to be travelling with a load of devices, consider taking a splitter or other adapter with several outlets.

Finances

As a good member of the EU, Portugal is part of the euro zone, which reduces the mental exertion from converting amounts in your head if you're from another Eurozone country.
One point to note: don't forget to find out from

your bank if additional charges apply to foreign transactions.

But there's also good news, as the low cost of living in Portugal will let you save on your basic expenses and allow a few treats such as restaurant visits and activities.

In terms of daily life

Depending on the region, you will often find that bars, cafes, restaurants and tourist organizations won't accept credit cards, or their card payment terminal doesn't recognize foreign credit cards. We therefore recommend that you always have some cash on you as you travel around.

There are lots of banks and cash machines; you can find them pretty much everywhere. But be warned that some local banks may charge a fee for withdrawals.

Tipping is not mandatory in Portugal but it is appreciated. Tips are usually about 5 to 10 per cent of the total bill.

To help you get an estimated budget for your camper van trip to Portugal, we've listed some amounts (in round numbers) based on our experience travelling around for two months, with Paris as the point of departure:

- Fuel: €1,200 (driving about 8,600 km)
- Road tolls: €260

During our two-month adventure, we spent about **€58 per day**.

Petrol: €19
Tolls: €4
Shopping: €15
Restaurants: €8
Refreshments (cafes, bars, cake shops): €5
Campsites and vehicle rest areas: €3
Hotels: €2
Other expenses (souvenirs, parking, etc.): €2

Some further details to help you interpret these numbers. On the one hand, when it came to food and drink expenditure we didn't hold back given that this is a country with lots of temptations for gastronomists. On the other hand, the money we spent on shelter (campsites, hotels) needs to be put in perspective as we were travelling in the mid-season and low season for the tourist industry. The rates and prices given in this guide are only indicative and you may find they are different when you set off on your own adventure!

Also, our trip of 8,600 km in two months might not be representative for your route or your average consumption.

The itinerary

To start with the obvious: much of your road trip will be spent on the road. And even if this is an inherent part of the adventure, it's not

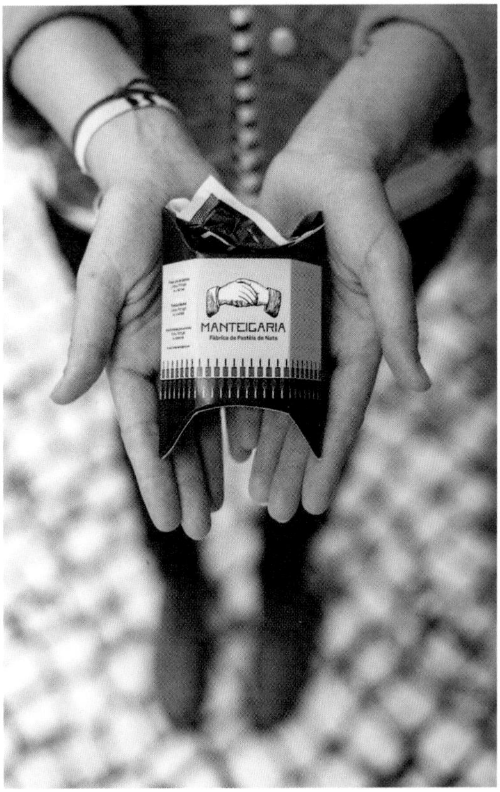

necessarily the main objective. So you need to decide on an effective itinerary. In our case, we perused numerous guides, blogs and books on Portugal just to be sure we didn't miss anything out (and to include areas that are less well known) and to let us be as comprehensive as possible when drawing up a basic route for our journey. You might not have as much time as we did, so this book should be useful in helping you choose and create your own customized adventure! After all, even if a camper van road trip is partly an opportunity for spur-of-the-moment detours, doing plenty of preparation before setting off will let you make the most of your time when you're there and get the maximum out of your holiday!

We used two very handy tools to transfer our basic plan onto a map: the Planificateur À Contresens tool (in French only) and Mapstr. When you start working out a general route for your journey, these tools or similar ones will make your job a lot easier. That's particularly true for a country like Portugal where you will be tempted to add more and more stages, whether for cultural, historical or recreational outings.

Planificateur À Contresens is an interactive map but – unlike Google Maps – there's no limit on the number of stages you can use (which is actually quite important when planning a two-month road trip). The Planificateur À Contresens tool also lets you add notes to each stage so you don't forget anything, and calculate a budget, your carbon footprint, the overall number of kilometres and the distance between two stops. In short, it's our preferred tool and we're happy to share this tip with you!

As for Mapstr, it is a kind of community guide on a global scale that anyone can use to find out what's interesting to visit, the must-see places and where you should go/eat/sleep (or share that information if you want or feel the need to). You will often find useful feedback, contact details, opening hours and links to websites as well. You won't regret downloading this app! And for all those who still appreciate the touch and smell of paper, a good old-fashioned map never goes amiss (it's also nice to be able to trace your route with your finger and mark it as a memory)!

The playlist

Ah – the music! You can't have a successful road trip without a cool playlist. For those who need music when behind the wheel, you could create a playlist in advance to accompany you as you drive across Portugal!

We put together some amazing playlists, which have a pretty inexhaustible supply of tracks! Of course, this assumes you have a network connection or sufficient storage space on your phone to save all the tracks, or a selection of them.

Throughout the book, you'll find tracks at the bottom of the pages from the original musical backdrop to our own journey, numbers we will always associate with the fantastic scenery we drove through. If you want to join us in reliving the experience of this third edition of Drive Your Adventure, we invite you to listen to this playlist "DYA#3 — Exploring Portugal" on Deezer.

Portugal is a country with loads to offer and lots of variation, whether in its scenery, its historical and cultural heritage or the many activities you can do there. While you don't want to be stifled by too rigid a predefined programme, make sure you allocate your time effectively so you don't miss anything!

Equipment

As we said earlier, you can visit Portugal all year round because of its Mediterranean climate. Depending on the season you choose, some activities will be easier to do than others. Of course, your choice will affect what equipment you need to take. Swimmers will fill the camper van with their most impressive aquatic accessories, hikers will take boots suitable for all possible terrains and as for bowling aficionados – well, they may prefer to borrow their equipment on site.

Anglers, you won't want to be outdone so don't forget to take fishing equipment suitable for both sea fishing and freshwater fishing. As regards the former option, a quick Internet search will take you to the government site where you can apply for a permit, at least five days before the required validity start date (www.dgrm.mm.gov.pt/en/). The latter is something you arrange that when you get there. You need to go to an office of the Instituto da conservação da natureza e das florestas and pay a small fee in return for the magic permit (15 euros for seven days, 20 euros for thirty days or 50 euros for a calendar year).

As you undoubtedly already know, Portugal is one of the top European destinations, perhaps the top, for surfing beaches. You can easily hire the equipment locally but if you do plan to take your surfboard or stand-up paddle board, remember to fit a roof-rack on your van. That's also useful information for canoeing and kayaking fans as this fantastic country has loads of lakes and rivers.

For all you golfers out there, we haven't forgotten you and we'd definitely recommend clearing a space at the back of your van for your golf clubs. Portugal basically reigns supreme on Planet Golf, monopolizing the title of best destination in the world for golfing from 2014 to 2018.

So now we come to the big question: what do you need to take in your camper van? The answer will be slightly different for everyone depending on their habits, but we reckon there are five indispensable things:

1) Multimedia equipment: a camera, phone, laptop and so on for keeping a great record of your trip and sharing it. Having said that, there's nothing stopping you going totally offline and off-grid during your adventure.

2) Equipment for making coffee and/or tea. The Roammates really go for the portable 'cof-

fee dripper', as Clémence can't start the day without a cup of coffee.

3) A good pair of shoes for strolling around town and/or roaming the countryside, and a pair of flip-flops for the shower and the beach!

4) A small brush or broom for getting soil and/or sand out of the van at various points during the day. We wouldn't go without our traditional African broom made of palm leaves!

5) An Omnia camping oven. Since we've been travelling with this, there hasn't been anything we've been unable to concoct on board the van!

As regards everyday items, if you're intending to hire your fittings from WeVan, please note that the team will give you all the basic equipment you need such as kitchen utensils, fitted sheets or even a solar-powered shower. Going further, they can also offer you an extensive range of accessories and options such as roof-racks, roof boxes, waterless portable camping toilets or bike racks (yes, there are some great mountain bike tracks in Portugal).

More info in books and on the Internet

Although this travel book aims to be as comprehensive as possible to help you plan your camper van adventure, we've included a list of other publications and websites where you can find more detailed information. You can use them for making specific preparations (such as for hiking trips).

Bibliography:

Lonely Planet: for a more exhaustive list of buildings and useful addresses.
I Love the Seaside - Vol 1 Southwest Europe: for water sports fans.
Guide Tao (French only): for an ethical and more environmentally friendly trip.
Wild Guide: for the natural, secret and authentic Portugal.
Michelin Green Guide: for themed routes and itineraries.
Simplissime (French only): for the basic outline of your adventure and the must-sees.
Le Guide de conversation des enfants - Les Éditions Bonhomme de chemin (French only): a very good illustrated phrasebook for all the family, easily digestible and with all you need for a short visit to Portugal. It's small enough that you can take it everywhere.

Internet:

visitportugal.com: Portugal's official tourism site is well designed and very comprehensive, whatever topic you want to look up.
gotoportugal.eu: a multilingual blog with lots of great ideas, often away from the main tourist spots.
rotavicentina.com: its interactive map lets you personalize your hikes along the Vicentina Coast.
viaalgarviana.org: a complete description of the Via Algarviana from east to west and the many routes that cross it.
portugaleasycamp.com: an early example of Portuguese agritourism. The site gives a list of farms (farm = quinta, herdade) where you can spend the night in your motorhome. It had only just been set up when we wrote this book and didn't have all that many addresses, but the quality of the accommodation already online, our contacts with the founders and the website design have convinced us this is a promising venture!
park4night.com: our partner gives detailed, illustrated and extensive reviews of spots where you could spend the night or stop during the day, service areas, campsites and so on.
Mapstr, Planificateur à Contresens and **Google Maps** for defining and refining your itinerary.

Making a success of your Portuguese adventure

Outdoor activities in Portugal

Sandwiched between a famous Atlantic coastline and mountain ranges and parks that deserve to be better known, Portugal is one big playground with tons of activities you can do under your own steam or with a guide. For example, you could:

• Sunbathe on one of the many beaches as you enjoy a well-earned rest.

• Go surfing, of course, because whatever your level there will be waves somewhere of just the right size.

• Go hiking, cycling or horse-riding, whether in one of the country's many nature parks or its only national park or elsewhere.

• Go out on a lake or hit the waves in a kayak or on a stand-up paddle board.

• Complete eighteen holes on one of the peninsula's many splendid golf courses.

• Go skiing down the country's highest peaks.

• Go fishing in freshwater or the sea.

We'll leave you to add to this list!

Some ideas for pacing your journey

While some regions are more appealing during the high season, social and cultural life in Portugal doesn't drop down a gear during the winter months. There is always something going on somewhere, whether it's a religious festival or civic event, a traditional market or a themed fair!

Even in February, there are things to see everywhere. Throughout the country, that month is marked by carnival celebrations, with festivities in vivid colours. In some regions, the fun can stretch out over several months, for example in the town of Bragança

which lights up from December to February. If you're visiting in the winter, don't miss the processions of Loulé, Nazaré or even Lisbon itself.

Continuing on this subject, here are some festivals and events with a range of themes that won't fail to enrich your adventure:

• *Essência do Vinho*, Porto, end of February: a wine fair where more than 300 producers from all over the country compete with one another in the grand setting of the Palácio da Bolsa.

• *Festival Internacional de Chocolate de Óbidos*, late April – early May: exhibitions, tastings and workshops with just one star: chocolate.

• *Festa do Mar, Nazaré*, first Sunday in May: parade of fishing boats in the harbour, procession of floats through the town's streets and all kinds of festivities in honour of the patron saints of fishermen.

• *Rota do Petisco do Algarve*, throughout May: from Odeceixe to Cabanas de Tavira, large numbers of businesses, the petiscadores, take part, letting you explore the best gastronomic specialties the region has to offer. The principle: at each place, you get one dish and one glass of wine for just 3 euros.

• *Fado no Castelo*, Lisbon, mid-June: three days of fado concerts within the walls of Castelo de São Jorge.

• *Festival Med*, Loulé, end of June: a programme of music and cuisine from around the world in the town's historic centre, plus a sprinkling of dance and street theatre.

• *Super Bock Super Rock*, Meco, mid-July: one of the country's biggest music festivals with rock, indie and hip-hop. It is even possible to get an all-inclusive pass and camp out under the pine trees with your van.

• *Gliding Barnacles*, Figueira da Foz, late August – early September: four to seven days, depending on the year, with surfing, food, arts & crafts, music and even improvised mini-concerts on the beach.

• *Festival Nacional de Gastronomia de Santarém*, late October – early November: Portugal's best restaurateurs represent their regions and present local products with the aim of advertising the rich gastronomic diversity of the country.

• *Rota dos Petiscos e Vinhos do Alentejo*, Lisbon: for fifteen days stretching from April into May, the chefs at about ten restaurants spread across the capital work closely with a wine grower in Alentejo chosen in advance so that they can perfect one or two petiscos (snacks) in perfect harmony with the wine. €4.50 for the petisco plus a glass of the associated Alentejo wine.

This list is obviously not exhaustive so don't hesitate to dig further. Good starting points are the municipal and tourist office websites for the towns you plan to pass through, so you can add some more items to your itinerary!

Getting to Portugal in a camper van

While this can be a major question for other countries across the sea from France, the problem of how to get to Portugal from France is pretty easy to solve. You get in your camper van, input the Portuguese town of your choice in your satnav and off you go. Congrats, you've reached Portugal!
Sure, there's a time lag between getting in the van and crossing the border – possibly quite a big lag, depending where you start from.

Obviously you're not likely to be going there from Paris like we did, but the relative extra distances may help you decide. So here's a mini-summary of the distances from Paris via the different routes:

• Chazemais – Bragança: 1,130 km
• Chazemais – Porto: 1,370 km
• Chazemais – Lisbon: 1,520 km
• Chazemais – Faro: 1,710 km

Why Chazemais? Because this little village is well known (yes, it really is well known in France) for being the geographical centre of

the country. That makes it ideal for readers of this guide wanting to calculate distances if passing through France.

The Portuguese road network

The Portuguese network will look familiar to anyone used to driving in France, for example, with its motorways, secondary roads and so on. Most of the roads are also of a high standard, so your suspension won't suffer, and it's easy to find service stations in all regions, even deep in the countryside.

Such a good road network also makes it very easy to drive from one end of Portugal to the other: the diagonal route Bragança – Sagres (about 800 km) takes seven hours!
Portuguese motorways are toll roads. You will come across two kinds of toll systems:

• The classic toll stations where you take a ticket at the entrance and pay at the exit (credit card or change, but make sure you don't get in the lane with a big 'V' on the sign, as that's reserved for subscribers to the Via Verde electronic toll system).
• Electronic toll stations.

These aren't complicated. You just have to go to the toll card website (www.tollcard.pt/) and follow the instructions step by step. Basically, you register your van's number plate and add prepaid credit for it using cards worth 5, 10, 20 or 40 euros, which you can buy online. These prepaid cards can also be bought locally at Portuguese post offices, which your satnav will give as CTT Correios de Portugal.
All the info you need can be found at www.portugaltolls.com.

Driving

As in other European countries:

• Children under 12 are not allowed in the front passenger seat.
• Pedestrians have right of way on the road.
• Phoning while driving is banned.
• The permitted maximum blood alcohol level for drivers is 0.5 g/l, but when in doubt, don't drink before driving!
• All vehicles must have a high-vis jacket and a warning triangle.

While these rules are the same in most countries, others are different, such as the maximum speeds: 120 km/h for the motorways, 100 km/h for dual carriageways, 90 km/h on trunk roads and 50 km/h in built-up areas.
Those are the basic rules and they will probably seem very familiar. Even so, we advise you to be very alert when you are on the road as Portuguese driving can involve some rather 'surprising' manoeuvres. The average driver has a liberal interpretation of the priority rules, drives very fast, tailgates you and overtakes you in what sometimes seem to be impossible situations. In short, you need to be prepared for a Formula 1 style of driving. But breathe deeply and you'll be fine.

Campsites in Portugal

Bad news for people who like spending the night in the middle of nature: 'wild' camping is banned in Portugal (although it's apparently tolerated depending on the season and region). On the other hand, there are alternatives that mean you don't have to spend every night at a campsite.
Of course, there's nothing wrong with a few nights at campsites – it lets you air your equipment and benefit from modern comforts.
That's good because Portugal has a very wide range of sites on offer.

Wherever you are in the country, you'll have no difficulty finding an affordable campsite or a rest area for camper vans with showers and other sanitary facilities. Some of these rest areas are even provided free of charge by the local municipality. In short, you won't experience any particular problems finding somewhere to spend the night!

Food

The first thing to note based on our first-hand observations: Portuguese cuisine is as rich and varied as its towns and regions! The Portuguese enjoy grilled meat and fish, home-style dishes, pastries, a wide range of breads and so on. In other words, it wouldn't be a good idea to pick your trip to the land of Magellan as the time to go on a diet.

Note that in restaurants you pay extra for appetizers (amuse-bouches as you come in, bread, butter, olives, pâté and so on), even if they were brought without you ordering them; this isn't necessary a devious ploy, it's simply the standard practice. Of course you have the right to refuse them. It's also obligatory to specify these extras in the menu along with their price; if that isn't the case and you ate them without being informed, you also have the right to refuse to pay. What is more, the bread is usually billed as an extra. On the same subject, the Portuguese don't drink tap water so you'll be served a small or large bottle of water and then billed for it. Once again, this is just the standard practice, not a ploy to trap tourists.

As for local specialties, well, you won't know which to try first. Whether we are talking cheeses, charcuterie, wines of all colours, pastries both sweet and savoury, bread or empadas, you will be spoilt for choice. There are too many of them to list them here, but you will be able to find them in supermarkets, mercearias, food markets, cooperatives or farm shops. Note that large supermarkets also sell food products that are typical for that region or district; these can mostly be found in the bread, pastry and delicatessen sections. The fruit and veg are also usually locally grown and seasonal too. Okay, we weren't going to make a list but here's one anyway to give you some idea of the products that added flavour to our meals:

- *empadas de frango* from Lidl, these mini chicken pies are absolutely delicious and less than 1 euro each
- *queijo da Serra*, a cheese from the Serra da Estrela area (but it can be found all over the country)
- more generally, *queijos curados* (matured cheeses)
- various spicy sausages (*chouriços*), to be eaten cold or cooked
- *galão*, the Portuguese equivalent of the latte macchiato!
- *pastéis de nata*, custard puff pastries that are usually good wherever you are, provided they are fresh
- bread – each region or even town has its own recipe
- a thousand and one local wines, with a special mention for the Moscatel, a syrupy dessert wine from the Douro not unlike a French Muscat.

That should get you properly prepared!

Language tips for the journey

Alphabet and pronunciation

We'll start with some details of the pronunciation.

An 'e' at the start of a word is silent when followed by an 's'

The 'u' is pronounced 'u' as in flu

The 's' is pronounced 'sh' as in hash

The 'x' is pronounced 'z' as in zoo

The 'nh' is pronounced 'ny' as in canyon

The 'ão' is pronounced 'a-u'

They roll their r's!

An indispensable word: *Pastel de nata* (pas-tèl de nata) / *Pastéis de nata* in the plural (pas-teïsh de na-ta)!

N.B. the stress is often on the final syllable.

Some basic words and phrases

Hello: *Olà! / Bom Dia* (bon di-ya - a French nasal "bon") / *Boa tarde* (bo-a tarde) / *Boa noite* (bo-a noï-te)
Goodbye: *Adeus* (adé-ush)
Please: *Por favor* (por fa-vor)
Thank you: *Obrigado* if you're a guy (o-bri-ga-du) / *Obrigada* if you're a girl
Thank you very much! *Muito obrigado* or *obrigada* (muy-tu)
Excuse me: *Desculpe* (desh-cul-pe)
Sorry: *Com licença* (kon li-senn-za)
My name is ...: *Chamo-me...* (sha-mume)
How do you say...? *Como se diz...?* (ko-mu se dish...?)
Where are the toilets?: *Onde é a casa de banho?* (ondee ee a ka-za de ba-nyu)
How much does that cost? *Quanto custa isto?* (kuan-tu kush-ta ish-tu?)
I don't understand: *Não compreendo* (na-u kon-prien-du)
I don't speak Portuguese: *Não falo português* (na-u fa-lu por-tu-guesh)
Straight on: *Sempre em fente* (sempreh en frenn-teh)
Go left: *À esquerda* (a shkerda)
Go right: *À direita* (a direï-ta)
Monday / Tuesday / Wednesday / Thursday / Friday / Saturday / Sunday: *Segunda-feira* (s-gun-da feï-ra) / *Terça-feira* (ter-sa feï-ra) / *Quarta-feira* (kuar-ta feï-ra) / *Quinta-feira* (kinn-ta feï-ra) / *Sexta-feira* (seïsh-ta feï-ra) / *Sábado* (sa-ba-du) / *Domingo* (do-min-gu)
What's the time?: *Que horas são?* (que orash sa-u)
I would like ...: *Eu queria...* (ee-u kee-ria...)
I'm looking for ...: *Procuro* (pro-ku-ro)
It's delicious: *É delicioso!* (ee dee-li-sio-zo)
Enjoy your meal: *Bom apetite!* (bon a-pe-ti-teh)
I'm allergic: *Sou alérgico(-a)* (so aler-gi-ku(-a))
Bless you! *Santinho!* (san-ti-nyu)

But don't worry, we nearly always managed to communicate somehow, whether in English, French or a few bastardized Portuguese words or as a last resort, miming what we were looking for! Based on our experiences, the Portuguese throughout the country (with the possible exception of the Algarve) are incredibly kind and generous when it comes to offering help or giving information. They don't begrudge you their time and will never abandon you before finding a solution.

Checklist for your road trip

Before you set off

- ☐ Draw up an itinerary (or list of must-sees)
- ☐ Download Park4Night
- ☐ Make playlists
- ☐ Check health advice
- ☐ Same for pets
- ☐ Check levels
- ☐ Check tyre pressures
- ☐ Check lights and indicators

Paperwork

- ☐ Passport (and visas if necessary)/national ID card
- ☐ Driving licence
- ☐ Car registration certificate
- ☐ Travel assistance insurance card (and policy number)
- ☐ Camper van manual
- ☐ European Health Insurance Card
- ☐ Transport reservations
- ☐ Credit/debit card

Equipment for the van

- ☐ Paper maps and/or GPS
- ☐ Spare tyre in good condition
- ☐ Emergency breakdown kit
- ☐ Torch
- ☐ Ice scraper
- ☐ Car sunshade (windscreen and rear and side windows)
- ☐ Mini toolbox

Everyday items

- ☐ Duvet or quilt (or both, depending on the season)
- ☐ Pillows
- ☐ Blanket
- ☐ Camping cable adapter (with CEE label) + extension
- ☐ Cafetière/kettle/mugs (enamel + insulated)
- ☐ Omnia camping stove
- ☐ Crockery, aluminium cooking utensils
- ☐ Toilet bag
- ☐ First aid kit
- ☐ Notebook, pencil, pen
- ☐ Sunglasses and soft cloths
- ☐ Sun cream
- ☐ Mosquito repellent
- ☐ Biodegradable or reusable wipes
- ☐ Toilet paper
- ☐ Tea-towels
- ☐ Terry towels and/or microfibre towels
- ☐ Rubbish bags
- ☐ Handkerchiefs
- ☐ Small brush
- ☐ Cigarette lighter

- ☐ Washing line
- ☐ Swiss army knife
- ☐ Reusable bottles
- ☐ Duckboard (for the shower)
- ☐ Flip-flops (also for the shower!)
- ☐ Fold-away table and chairs
- ☐ Pack of cards and mini board games
- ☐ Sleeping masks and wax earplugs
- ☐ Umbrella
- ☐ Small spade
- ☐ String shopping bag
- ☐ Big shopping bags for the market
- ☐ Small spice set

Outdoor gear

- ☐ Walking/hiking boots
- ☐ Multi-purpose waterproof jacket
- ☐ Thin padded jacket
- ☐ Sportswear tops (to vary the layers)
- ☐ Hiking trousers + rainproof overtrousers
- ☐ Swimsuit (or tri suit!)
- ☐ Flasks
- ☐ Rucksack
- ☐ Headlamp
- ☐ Hammock and/or Lamzac
- ☐ Skiing/surfing/diving/fishing gear
- ☐ Paddles/canoe/kayak

Multimedia equipment

- ☐ Smartphone
- ☐ Camera/lenses/waterproof case
- ☐ Dashboard camera
- ☐ SD cards
- ☐ Tripod
- ☐ Portable computer
- ☐ Tablet
- ☐ Hard disk
- ☐ Set of cables/chargers/multi-socket adaptors
- ☐ Travel battery
- ☐ E-reader

En route

- ☐ Always have some cash on you
- ☐ Always keep an eye on the petrol gauge
- ☐ Look out for places to get some shut-eye
- ☐ Drive sensibly
- ☐ Drive on the right
- ☐ Sing at the top of your voice
- ☐ Be good citizens
- ☐ Enjoy the scenery

Have a great trip!

Along the Douro

It's nearly 28 September, the date we are due to set off on our Lusitanian (i.e. Portuguese) adventure. It's the day we've spent four months preparing for, months in which we drew up the best possible itinerary and contacted loads of people to organize meet-ups and activities, all so that this guide would be as comprehensive as possible.

For this voyage, we collected a brand-new Marco Polo from the Mercedes-Benz France offices and drove back down along the River Ariège to polish off the final details, break in our new equipment and so forth. and figure out what we should call our camper van! After an animated discussion, we decided on Fernão, the first name of the Portuguese explorer Magellan. Clémence, Thomas, Nel and Fernão: now the gang's all here.

Finally, our departure date has arrived! We set off from the camper van trade fair Salon du Véhicule de Loisirs, cheered on by a delirious crowd. (OK, largely made up of friends and the WeVan and Mercedes teams, but delirious nonetheless.) After driving for about fifteen hours, we cross the Spanish-Portuguese border. Portugal, here we come!

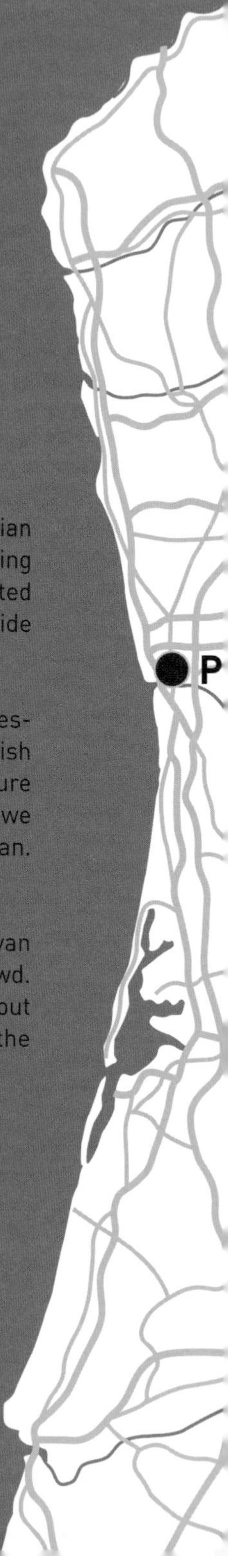

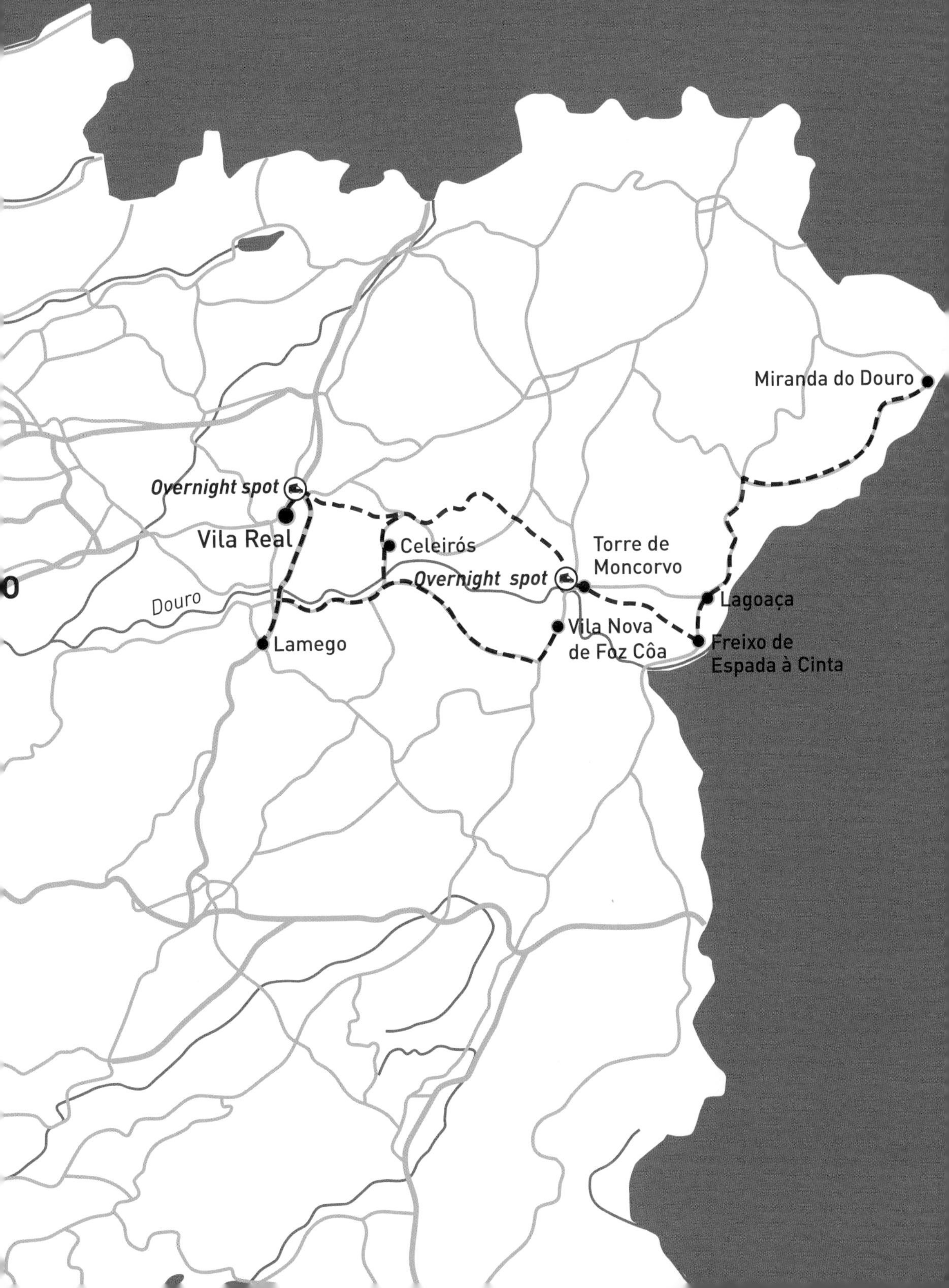
Miranda do Douro
Overnight spot
Vila Real
Celeirós
Torre de Moncorvo
Overnight spot
Lagoaça
Douro
Vila Nova de Foz Côa
Freixo de Espada à Cinta
Lamego

Paddling down the Douro

For our first encounter with Portugal, we decided on the little town of Miranda do Douro and the Douro International Natural Park. Located in the north-east of the country, this little town is not on the international tourist radar. But there is nothing ordinary about its history and our guide for the day, Pedro Cordeiro, enjoys regaling us with some fascinating details.

One aspect in particular will catch your eye – or ear (given that like us, you will have been revising your Portuguese before starting your trip): the locals in Miranda don't speak Portuguese to one another, they speak Mirandese, which was recognized as an official language in 1999 and is the only other official language in the country. Here's how!

Well, towards the end of the eighteenth century the European monarchies were not exactly on the best of terms. In other words, there were wars going on everywhere. Portugal and Spain were no exception and in 1762 Spain decided to invade its neighbour, attacking (you guessed it) Miranda do Douro. Although thought virtually impregnable, the town still fell after the gunpowder stored in the castle exploded, destroying a third of the place to create a way through. A few years later, the bishop of Miranda fled the town for the splendour of Bragança, taking with him all the riches of the diocese. Miranda never recovered; it had to wait nearly two centuries before it could rise again from the ashes thanks to the construction of several dams in the River Douro. This isolation for two centuries explains why the town has such a distinctive culture!

We're in luck because Pedro turns out to be an inexhaustible source of information on this topic. During the off-season, he's an ornithologist who liaises with wind farm operators to make sure migrating birds don't experience any problems in the south of the country. But he is also (and most importantly as far as we are concerned) the only kayaking guide in Miranda do Douro.

After a morning of discussions and taking care of business, we meet him at the edge of the water before setting off for a few hours paddling along the bottom of the splendid canyon carved out by the Douro. The river forms a natural border between Portugal and Spain as it meanders past amazing cliffs coloured by lichen and inhabited by various species of eagle and even black storks. The rhythm is relaxed, Pedro is a joy to listen to, while he also takes

First Day of My Life - Bright Eyes

the time to pick up bits of rubbish floating around.

We totally recommend calling on the services of We totally recommend calling on the services of our new friend (30 euros per person for our trip). You won't regret your time with this nature lover and advocate for his region. He can take you out on the water or along the local tracks in his 4×4, on foot or on bike to show you the area or go bird spotting. It's a must!

Douro Pula Canhada

Cais Fluvial, 5210-000 Miranda do Douro

Pedro is the only kayak guide in Miranda do Douro and for this section of the river. Best period for kayaking trips: May to October. Specialized in trips for a few friends or family (larger groups accepted). Outdoor shower available for use on arrival!

Overnight spots in Portugal

Camping 'in the wild' is banned in Portugal, whether you are doing so in the countryside, on private land or in natural parks (where punishments are harsher). However, a converted van can spend the night in a parking place on two conditions:
• There must be no sign saying overnight parking is prohibited.
• The camper van mustn't be bigger than the parking space.

However, normal camping practices are not tolerated at all. So you won't be able to put out tables and chairs or set up the awning wherever you are parked (excluding campsites of course).
For the first few nights, you are advised to get to your spot during daytime to help you get your bearings. Make sure your spot is legal, quiet and flat. Whether it's a parking area on the edge of a forest or park or close to a beach, next to a harbour office or even in a quiet side street, always make sure you won't be disturbing the locals and check there aren't any signs banning parking entirely or during certain times (on market days, for example). Finally, don't park in front of an outdoor seating area or shop window or somewhere that obstructs the view from a home.
There are lots of digital tools to help you find suitable spots. There's the indispensable Park4Night to get other travellers' advice on a spot, Google Maps and its extension Street View to locate that rare gem using aerial view, or various social networks (especially Instagram) where vanlifers share their plans with pictures and GPS coordinates.

If you're not sure, if there's a storm brewing or you're just very tired, it may not be very glamorous but you can always find refuge in a supermarket car park. Many chains, such as Intermarché or Continente, have special parking spaces with a few key services (launderette, discharge of dirty water and blackwater, refilling your drinking water tank and so on).

Hunting for lookout points

We're only one day into our Portugal adventure and we've already been able to admire the beauty of the Douro International Natural Park from the water. In addition to our kayaking trip, our guide also took us to a miradouro, or lookout point in English, the São João das Arribas, perched a few dozen metres above the river.

It's a magnificent site that has been occupied since the Stone Age. You can also still clearly see traces of structures from the Roman Empire. You can also find a chapel there, which is obviously more recent. On Pedro's advice, we now plan to go hunting for more of these famous miradouros tomorrow. Many of these lookout points are little known and some only became official just before the summer of 2019. No matter, we'll manage to track them down!

So we follow the path of the Douro (at a distance) driving along the N221, deviating now and then to take in some cliffs. Which was not always an easy matter! Take the example of the lookout point in Picote, a tiny village with very narrow streets. We'd advise parking in the church square (or Largo da Igreja for language purists) and then continuing on foot. The walk will take you five minutes and you won't regret it.

If you think the views from Picote were dazzling, you will love what comes next! The viewpoints come fast and furious almost without interruption as we drive south along the N221. Without listing them all, we were particularly impressed by the miradouros of Cruzinha, Carrascalinho (spectacular in the fading light of the day!) and Penedo Durão, all accessible by road. Even if 'road' sometimes means no more than a dirt track... but nothing our trusty Fernão can't cope with. But here too, it was definitely worth the effort.

Great addresses we found

Area de servicio para autocaravanas

Torre de Moncorvo
41°10'51.2"N | 7°02'29.6"W

A small, well run site for motorhomes, camper vans and even classic campers, with a large grass area for people to pitch their tents. It's laid out in terraces like the surrounding vineyards. The sanitary facilities are basically clean, a few electric sockets are available (depending on how busy it is), there's water, bins, somewhere to empty your tank, the municipal Wi-Fi – everything you need for a very affordable zero euros: you can stay at this site free of charge!

Gruta Nossa Senhora de Lourdes

Sanfins do Douro
41°17'31.1"N | 7°30'51.7"W

It's a little weird, but this little parking spot where we decided to spend the evening has a small cave containing a religious statue. Presumably Our Lady of Lourdes, given the name of the place. Whatever; this spot on the west-facing hillside gives a nice view of the valley and we were able to enjoy a totally amazing sunset in reds and oranges. You could almost spend the night there!

Overnight spot

41°10'38.55"N | 7°6'45.976"W

La Praia Fluvial de Foz do Sabor

If you're looking for a great place to spend a sunny day, go for a swim or enjoy some aquatic sports, there's no need to look any further! The Praia Fluvial de Foz do Sabor, at the point where the Sabor and Douro rivers meet, is ideal for you. With its vast stretches of greenery, clear water, barbecues and water tap points available for all, it is also the ideal spot for blowing up your stand-up paddling board by hand. Well, it's a long story.

And if blowing up your SUP board ever takes you all day and you get caught by surprise by the setting sun, this attractive little riverside beach is just the place to spend the night! It means you will be able to dip your feet in the water in the morning, take advantage of the sanitary facilities (under Café Sabor) and eat your breakfast with a lovely view of the river.

The quinta as a home from home

It's Thursday 3 October and we've made our plans. After a day off yesterday, we will be doing a big loop through the Douro valley, famous for its vineyards (a detail that will be important later). On the programme are some beautiful sun-baked routes, views of the Douro and a full tank of fuel. In short, non-stop happiness.

But it doesn't take long for our plans to get derailed after we stop off in the little town of Sabrosa, one of several places that claim to be the birthplace of Fernão de Magalhães. Of course we couldn't pass up an opportunity to pay homage to the famous navigator Magellan and the namesake of our faithful four-wheeled steed! A few photos later, we are just about to get in our camper van to set off again when we are accosted by Alfredo Martins, a cultural officer at the town hall, who offers to give us some information about the region. Our stickers aroused his curiosity. It seems our programme is set to be extended.

Naked As We Came - Iron & Wine

Alfredo has a lot to say to us, especially as he is delighted to be able to practice his French. Just as well for us, as we haven't made too much progress with our Portuguese during our first three days. In fact, you might even say some of us, starting from level zero, have regressed... We ask him if he knows any wine growers who we could drop in on and take some impromptu photos. One phone call later, and after pushing various leaflets into our hands on interesting places in the local area, he sends us to the Quinta (literally a farm) do Bucheiro.

That's when the day takes an extremely improbable turn. After ringing the doorbell, we are met by an elderly gent who turns out to be the husband of the lady who owns the place, Maria da Conceição. That name won't mean anything to you, nor did it to us. But it transpires that Maria is (if our calculations are right) the great-great-great-granddaughter of Dr Joaquim Pinheiro de Azevedo Leite Pereira. Another name that won't mean anything to you and didn't to us. But this doctor was quite simply the man who saved the winegrowing industry in Douro from certain death in the nineteenth century by grafting local grape varieties ravaged by Phylloxera (a kind of aphid) onto American vine rootstocks. Founded in 1751, Quinta do Bucheiro was literally the saviour to which all the other quintas in the region owe their survival.

Our host, Antonio Dias Teixeira, continues his tour of the place, from the cellar to the function room via the chapel and the small family museum, where his portrait hangs next to that of the business's founder and a portrait of the doctor. Why?
Because it is thanks to Antonio that the local wines are labelled as Douro wines rather than

Porto wines: he was the person who got the laws changed to allow the region to export its wines without having to go through Porto. It would not be a cliché to call our host a pioneer. This day is full of surprises.

But the history of the place and the revolution that Antonio initiated are just anecdotes in the final analysis. What will remain with us above all is the generosity of our hosts. Because while we are wandering from room to room and exploring the vineyards, Maria (now Nina to us) has secretly prepared a meal for us! We take our places at the table in the family's kitchen with Antonio and Nina to enjoy Feijocas do Douro, a dish of broad beans cooked in a local sauce (totally delicious), followed by pork spareribs with roast potatoes. All this was, of course, washed down with some of their own wines (in moderation, a habit we have once again slipped into our luggage).

The day we were supposed to be spending on our own on the road turned out to be full of interesting encounters: warm, sincere and authentic. We felt quite emotional as we drove off (with a few bottles in the back), bringing this enchanting episode to a close.

Casa do Bucheiro

Rua de São Caetano 87,
5060-024 Celeirós

To visit the estate, and taste and buy a few bottles of their excellent Douro DOC wines. You can also arrange and book reservations for a meal at the *quinta*.

The advantages of travelling in a converted van

- The freedom to explore an area at your own pace.
- Easy to meet locals, as they will be as curious as you are.
- Open the van doors to experience great social moments with other travellers sharing the rest area or campsite.
- For sporty types, it's easy to transport your equipment and you can get out there to do your activity right from the break of day.
- Sleep surrounded by nature – you can't imagine a better neighbour.
- Look out on different scenery nearly every morning as you drink your coffee, hot chocolate or tea.
- This mode of travel offers a real break and change of scene, and very different perspectives to a sedentary life.
- Reduce your daily life to the essentials, slow down and live in the moment.
- Varied settings as you move easily from countryside to town in a van that is pretty similar in size to a car.

Driving past the Douro vineyards

We have spent 15 packed hours when we finally say goodbye to our hosts Nina and Antonio of the Quinta do Bucheiro. Rather later than we intended for our big loop round the Douro valley, but meeting this couple has totally revitalized us. Whatever – off we go!

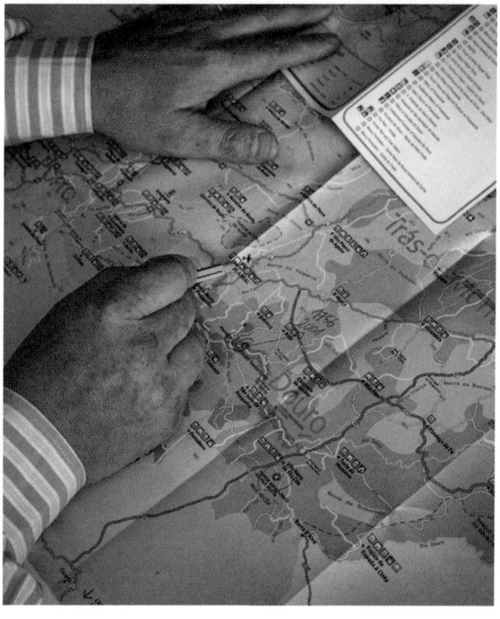

The circuit we are about to do starts – and ends, given that it's a loop – in Sabrosa. We start by heading south on the N323, a road that winds its way along the hillsides past terraced vineyards, scenery typical of this region (much of which has been classed a UNESCO world heritage site). We drive for kilometres along this lovely route before descending into the small town of Pinhão, our first stop. Partly to fill up but mainly to take some photos of the train station's azulejos, blue ceramic tiles decorating the building on the theme of the grape harvest.

♫ Into the Sun - Sons of the East

We then turn off east onto the N222, driving along the River Douro towards Peso da Régua. The road follows the bends in the river, lit up by the late afternoon sun. It's nearly 27 kilometres and 93 bends of pure joy offering views of vineyards, numerous quintas and other whitewashed houses, all of which earned the N222 the title of best route in the world in 2015. No less! We take a detour to visit Lamego, famous for its sanctuary of Our Lady of Remedies, reached by climbing 600 steps, although we are a bit late in the day for a return trip.

Next, we head north to Vila Real, where we decide to cut the loop in two. It's not necessarily easy to find a spot for the night at the last minute but after stocking up on provisions, we opt for the Parque de Campismo de Vila Real. It's simple, clean and with a free choice of where to park (a long extension cable is recommended to make sure you have a socket within reach). OK, it's a bit noisy as it is in the town but it's also ideal for an aperitif and tapas under the pines, followed by a good night's sleep.

If you have time, the Casa de Mateus is considered the town's must-see attraction. It will have to wait for another day for us, though, as we need to get on and finish that loop taking us back to Sabrosa. A journey of about 130 kilometres past sunlit vines and the peacefully meandering River Douro – we thoroughly recommend this route!

Overnight spot

41°18'12.9"N | 7°44'12.5"W

Vila Real campsite

In Portugal, as in other countries, there are campsites and then there are campsites. You have functional, flat, smooth ones with clearly demarcated spots separated by hedges, for example. And you have wilder versions, perhaps even located in woodland like in Vila Real. Simple, clean and rustic despite its proximity to the town, the site is ideal for a stopover, especially given the lack of alternative sites near the town. You can park where you like, even among the trees if your vehicle can drive across that terrain (an extension cable and chocks will help too). After a few manoeuvres, all that is left for you to do is enjoy the evening with an aperitif and snacks under the pines and a good night's sleep.

The almonds of Foz Côa

Portugal is known for its wine, its olive oil, its cod and if you did your homework, you will also know that the country is a major producer of cork. But the east of Portugal also happens to be a significant almond growing area. Its capital is Vila Nova de Foz Côa, our next destination. Mention almonds and you immediately think of sweet pastries, but we wouldn't want to overshadow the pastéis de nata and cause a diplomatic incident in our first week. We need specialists who can give us some inspiration!
So we try the town's bakeries, cake shops and tea shops in search of someone who can tell us more about the world of almonds. We have difficulty making ourselves understood. One failure, another failure... and finally the light at the end of the tunnel! A lady sitting outside raises her hand, trying to make us understand that she might be able to help with her rudimentary knowledge of French and English. Silvia, who seems to know the whole town, collars everyone who passes in a loud voice until her friend Delfina, who speaks perfect French, joins us at our outdoor cafe table. So here we are sitting at our table, ready to immerse ourselves in the world of the almond.

Now that the language barrier has been solved, we finally discover that Silvia is a member of the upper Douro almond association. Fate is on our side once again! Delfina also explains to us that nearly everyone in Vila Nova has their own plot with some almond trees, harvests the almonds themselves (in September in Portugal) and then dries the shells, which can keep fresh that way for months on end. Off we go to her home: Delfina wants to show us how to open the almonds with a cunha, an implement typical of the town. She can crack open two kilos of almonds in just one hour! Which is just as well given the enormous sacks waiting to be processed (we have arrived at the end of the harvest season). Anyway, she also gives us a simple recipe that will let us produce grilled salted almonds later as an aperitif nibble on board Fernão.

We really have got lucky again. For despite the years she spent in France, Delfina is a genuine local and an active member of the community. She shows us the house where she was born and the amazing church, and ends by offering us a bag of almonds and a bottle of olive oil she pressed herself. Silvia is not to be outdone and as it is now evening, she drives us to a restaurant we wouldn't even have spotted (a churrasqueira called Maria dos Pitos). Seeing that we can't speak Portuguese, the other customers order for us and we end up eating like royalty in this rather humble-looking little restaurant. What a day!

Roasted almonds

Preparation

Boil a pan of water. Once the water is boiling, switch off the heat and put the almonds in the water. Leave them to soak for 10 minutes.

After this immersion, take the almonds out of the water and then you can peel them without any trouble!

Put the almonds on a plate or in your mini-oven designed for use on a portable stove.

Switch on the heat, salt the almonds, turn them occasionally, add more salt to taste. Add pepper, paprika, curry powder or any other spice as wished.

Move the almonds around a bit until they are golden and you're good to go!

Great addresses we found

Museu do Côa

Rua do Museu,
5150-610 Vila Nova de Foz Côa

This museum showcases the cave art in the Côa valley and offers guided tours to sites of Palaeolithic art in the region (reservation required). There is also a restaurant with a view of the terraced vineyards and the point where the rivers Côa and Douro meet. Awesome!
www.arte-coa.pt

Churrasqueira Maria dos Pitos

R. da Corredoura 28,
5150-574 Vila Nova de Foz Côa

Specializes in grilled meat. The famous restaurant recommended by Silvia. We're still talking about it!

At the heart of the country – inland Beiras

We've been following the meandering River Douro for five days now, from lookout points to hills studded with vineyards. Less than a week hugging the river and it's already time to leave it and start crossing Portugal from north to south.

So we're leaving the winegrowing lands of the upper Douro area for very different scenery, wilder and unjustly overlooked by tourists – a part of the country that we fall in love with from the first few kilometres because of the harsh landscape and we look forward to exploring it.
But even if you get a certain sense of desolation as you thread your way past the arid hills of Beira Alta, the centre of Portugal along the Spanish border is brimming with some amazing treasures, both historical and natural. From the fortified towns that held off Napoleon's armies to the highest peak in continental Portugal, this first half of our trip to the south is already pretty exciting.
Let's go exploring the heart of Portugal!

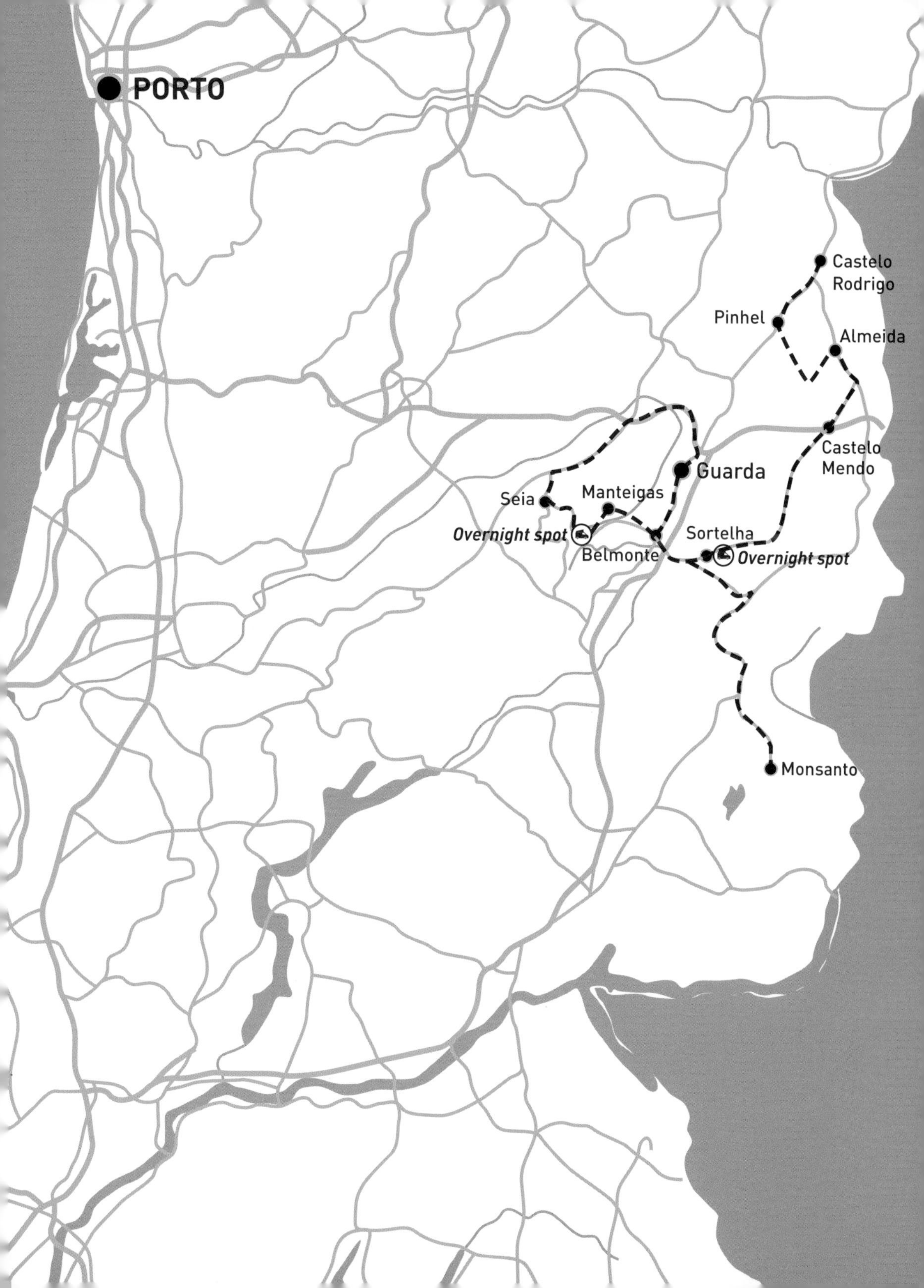
PORTO
Castelo Rodrigo
Pinhel
Almeida
Castelo Mendo
Guarda
Seia
Manteigas
Overnight spot
Belmonte
Sortelha
Overnight spot
Monsanto

The guardians of Beira Alta

It's time for us to leave Vila Nova de Foz Côa. After the miradouros and quintas, we are moving on to the castelos: we will be tracking down the ancient fortified towns of the Serra da Marofa. We head south-east to start with and the little town of Figueira de Castelo Rodrigo.

But we are mainly interested in Castelo Rodrigo, a separate village. With its fortress built in the Middle Ages, it was part of the line of defence along the Spanish border. It should be said that the history of this place and its neighbours was turbulent, to say the least. Nothing remains of the castle today except some ruins but the ancient town is quite well preserved. Its location on the top of a hill is really charming. If you want a view of the surrounding area, the panoramic vista from the Marofa lookout point is awesome!
From Castelo Rodrigo, the most 'logical' option would be for us to take the N332 going south to Almeida, our next stop. Except that the N221, to which we are now rather attached, apparently offers a breath-taking route (known as 'The Excommunicated') across the Serra da Marofa. Looks like we'll be making a detour! We don't regret that decision, as the route is bursting with amazing views. Even if we still don't understand how the route got its name...

When we get to Pinhel, we turn off east to get to Almeida. This journey isn't the most efficient route but it makes up for that in its beauty. We arrive in Almeida with its amazing

♫ *King And Lionheart - Of Monsters and Men*

ancient fortifications in the dying light of the day. Here too, there've been some twists and turns in the history of the place. The fortress played a significant role in the history of France, for instance. At a time when Napoleon Bonaparte was trying to isolate the English and when Portugal was a loyal ally of England and a strategic point on the continent, a trail of gunpowder from a poorly closed barrel caused the fortress's arsenal to explode, allowing the French troops to capture the town and gain a strong position.

A few kilometres further south, we climb up to the little village of Castelo Bom and its very narrow streets. While you can drive around the village, we still recommend leaving your vehicle below so that you don't disturb the quiet atmosphere.
A little further west, we are able to recycle our dehydrated bread by graciously offering it to

two charming donkeys grazing at the foot of the Castelo Mendo ramparts. It is all quite sublime as the setting sun drops to the horizon. In fact, we need to cut short our visit in order to get to Sortelha before nightfall. In vain. But the lights on the fortress give us some idea of the beauty of the place the next morning (see the overnight spot on the next page).

Anyway, we finish our tour of the guardians with Belmonte, another town with a castle in the centre on a hilltop. This list of Beira Alta's fortified towns is obviously not exhaustive but this quick general survey still gave us some idea of the region's rich history.

Overnight spot

40°19'48.1"N | 7°12'50.8"W

The fortress of Sorthela

To compensate for the general ban on wild camping, many Portuguese municipalities have decided to reserve a few parking spaces for RVs or to fit out rest areas and service stations for their use.

The little town of Sorthela has done a good job in this regard, allowing overnight parking at the foot of the fortress ramparts, high up a hill. Not only is this a peaceful spot to spend the night, it also offers awesome views of the surroundings and said fortress, which is backlit at night. This is an amazing spot and a must for anyone looking to spend the night in this area!

Serra da Estrela Natural Park

The Serra da Estrela mountain range and its park are located about two hours south-east of Porto. To learn more about this place, we head for Seia and CISE, which stands for Centro de Interpretação da Serra da Estrela. Waiting for us there are José and Tiago, who know the Serra like the back of their hand. They give us some key facts.

Did you know?

Covering an area of 1,010 square kilometres (60 km from north to south, 30 km from east to west), the Serra da Estrela Natural Park is not the most impressive It does nevertheless boast the highest point in continental Portugal, the Malhão da Estrela, 1993 metres high. The peak in question can be reached by road and it makes an excellent place to spend the night (see p. 62)!

The wildlife in the park is a relatively classic combination of wolves, foxes, deer, wild boar and otters. The roads are very good quality and are usually passable all year round. However, you should note that they might be closed when there is a snowfall. Although wild camping is not permitted along the dirt tracks, you can set up camp in parking areas inside the park (lookout points, car parks and so on). Of course you should use your discretion.

CISE

As the name suggests, CISE is an information centre where you will find all the information you need to prepare for your visit to the natural park. But that's not all! It also has an educational mission and programme, with seminars, exhibitions, bird-watching, films and so on.

José, Tiago and their colleagues are always ready to tell you about the treasures of the Serra da Estrela Natural Park, from the hiking trails to the most scenic routes and the best places to buy local products. What is more, many of the hiking trails are maintained by the centre's staff so they will be able to help you with all your questions about walking in the park (level of difficulty, viewing points, etc.).
Other activities such as canyoning, paragliding, climbing, water sports and even skiing, are possible in the park independently of CISE.

Local tradition

We talked about local products – a subject close to our hearts – earlier. We would specifically like to recommend the soft sheep's cheese in a washed rind, Queijo Serra da Estrela, a protected designation of origin. It's a real delight! You will also find more traditional cured meat specialties such as chorizo and hams.

The Serra da Estrela can hold its own in terms of textiles too, as a unique wool known as Burel is produced here, in Manteigas to be precise. It was brought back to life in 2010 thanks to two mountain lovers, João Tomás and Isabel Costa.

Finally, there is a breed of dog specific to the region, the cão da Serra da Estrela, literally the 'dog of the Serra da Estrela'. We found out from Suzette, whose dog breeding centre is renowned throughout the world, that these dogs with their impressive stature and thick coats are popular among shepherds because they are able to keep the wolves at bay. But perhaps not the most practical companion to take in your camper van...

Great addresses we found

Ti Branquinho

40°24'58.7"N | 7°35'22.1"W

Try one of Roberto's chorizo, cheese and/or cured ham sandwiches. Our tip: given their huge dimensions, start with one between you!

Vale do Rossim campsite

40°24'13.6"N | 7°35'17.7"W

Really cute campsite among the pine trees and close to the dam of the same name. Lots of hiking trails start near here.

Overnight spot

40°19'18.1"N | 7°36'55.6"W

Capela de Nossa Senhora do Ar

Sometimes called Torre in reference to the seven- metre tower at the summit (which, when added to the mountain's 1,993m, allows it to reach the symbolic threshold of 2,000 m), sometimes called Malhão da Estrela. Whatever its name, the site is well equipped (maybe too much so), with public toilets, a cafe with good-quality Wi-Fi, and even a small ski lift during the winter if you fancy donning your skis! Most importantly for us, there is a flat parking spot where we enjoyed spending the night, even if we did have to start up Fernão's heating system for once. Our tip: if the skies are clear, make sure you arrive at the summit in time for the sunset – you won't be disappointed!

Stopping off at tourist offices and interpretation centres

In addition to being a mine of information about the local area, they often have maps and street plans that are much more detailed than your basic GPS. You can go through them together depending on your interests. These specialists know the local roads and tracks like the backs of their hands and will be able to advise you on where you can go depending on the features of your converted van. They might also have some ideas for you about out-of-the-ordinary addresses and places to spend the night.
To track them down, search for turismo or centro de interpretação on the net.

Park highlights

We take off from Seia loaded with information leaflets. José and Tiago have added their own suggestions to the basic itinerary that we had planned, so that we get a good idea of the park in the two days that we have available.

We head along the N339 for Sabugueiro, a tiny village that also happens to be the highest in the country. An ideal place to buy some food and drink for the journey. If you see a cafe with old men in caps sitting outside, it's generally a good sign! We drive along the same road to the Lagoa Comprida dam. You could spend the night here, if you are discreet about it.

Suggested hikes, vol. 1:

There are two possible hikes starting at Lagoa Comprida. The first, an easy walk to the Covão dos Conchos dam, is 10 km there and back and mainly flat. The second is also not difficult with a climb of less than 200 m over a distance there and back of 7.8 km, which gets you to Lagoa Escura. From the car park, walk for 2 km with Lagoa Comprida on your right, then turn right onto a narrower path heading to Lagoa Escura. After 750 m, you will have to choose between an even narrower bridge (take care when crossing) and going round. A final kilometre will get you to your destination.

Continue on the route in the same direction until you get to the K26 boundary stone, then STOP!

Suggested hikes, vol. 2:

Two hikes start from K26. Here too, the first is easy. It takes you to Cântaro Gordo past some small lakes, ending with a great view of Lagoa dos Cantâros. The second is classed as difficult by our friends at CISE: it descends from the starting point at about 1,900 m to Loriga, 1,200 m lower down. And unless you've got someone to pick you up at the bottom, don't forget you'll need to climb back up (allow seven to eight hours for the return journey).

Another couple of hundred metres takes you to the highest point in the park – and the country – at 1,993m, offering both awesome views and an awesome place to spend the night!

To get back down, go back 200 m, then turn right for Manteigas. After we turn off onto the N338, the road takes us to Covão de Ametade, a pretty picnic spot among the trees a few metres from the parking area on the side of the road. It's well equipped with a stream running through it. It's also the starting point for various hiking and biking trails (see the signs explaining the routes) and you are allowed to pitch your tent there. Once we pass Covão da Ametade, we are on a section known as the Zêzere glacier valley road. It's quite narrow and winding, and you need to watch out as you're more than likely to come across a shepherd crossing the road with his flock of sheep or herd of goats. He may even offer to share the contents of his bag with you. If so, we recommend taking this opportunity for some impromptu bartering!

Next stop is Manteigas, which is ideal for getting in fresh supplies. Of fuel of course, but above all of cheeses and cured meats at the cafe-restaurant Serradalto, or fresh trout from the trout farm at the entrance to the town.

Once we have stocked up again, we take the N232 and stop off at the cafe Ti Branquinho. Enjoy a delicious chorizo, cured ham or cheese sandwich, or all three at once. We then turn left 200 m further along to head for the Vale do Rossim and the campsite of the same name. You can spend the night there (if you want) for 11 euros during the off-season. It has clean sanitation facilities, Wi-Fi throughout the site, parking spots in the shade of the pine trees, the option of sleeping in a yurt, etc. But above all, we have...

Suggested hikes, vol. 3:

From the campsite, walk to the lake and dam. At the end of the dam, look for the first post with a red stripe painted round it. Follow these red markers for about four hours on a long loop that will take you up the mountains surrounding the lake. A hike classed as medium, with spectacular views of the lake and even of the Malhão in the distance. It's the perfect way to end a visit to the park!

The heights of Monsanto

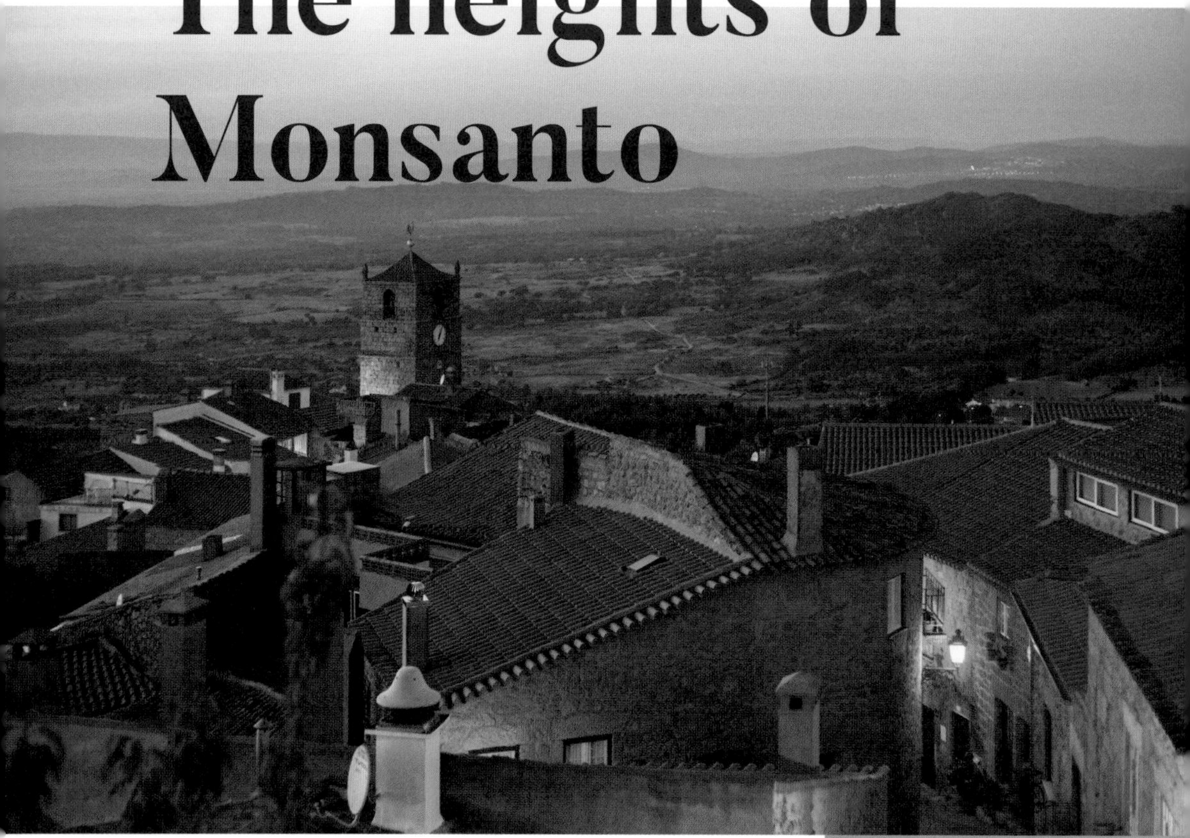

We would like to make clear from the start that this Monsanto has nothing to do with its American namesake. This one is much nicer and a far better option for food. The little village perched on a granite hill also makes an ideal stop between the Serra da Estrela and the Serra de São Mamede.

And it's a great place to walk around! The narrow paved streets that almost no vehicles dare go down are calm and offer pleasant shade in the afternoon heat. The village is unbelievably picturesque and definitely merits some time roaming its streets, or even savouring a glass of wine seated outside a cafe or dining there.

Mystery of Love - Sufjan Stevens

Great addresses we found

La Taverna Lusitana

R. do Castelo 19, 6060-091 Monsanto

A place that lives up to its name as you can either enjoy a drink there or eat a meal. We didn't sample the dishes (hot dishes, salads, platters, tapas and so on) but everything looked delicious, the manager was really nice and you will find all the usual drinks. But the real highlight of this place is its outdoor seating area, which we can't recommend highly enough. Built from wood and perched on a huge granite block, it looks out over the village, offering breath-taking views of both Monsanto and the surrounding plains. Unforgettable.

Petiscos & Granitos

R. do Castelo 16, 6060-091 Monsanto

Here too, the outdoor seating area is an oasis of calm. It's built on two levels like balconies looking out over the plain. This time, we did taste the dishes prepared by the kitchen; we focused on the petiscos, the Portuguese equivalent of tapas. Basically, they were to die for! It's not haute cuisine here, it's traditional country cooking, the kind of dishes that warm body and soul. Definitely not to be missed if you want to eat out in Monsanto. We particularly recommend the farinheiras com ovos mexidos, alheiras com ovo and migas a granitos.

Farinheiras com ovos mexidos

Ingredients for 4 people

2 farinheiras (smoked sausages)

6 eggs

1 large onion

Olive oil

Salt and pepper

Chives (optional)

Preparation

Peel the farinheiras and cut them into thick slices. Set aside.

Dice the onion and sauté it in a tablespoon of olive oil.

When the onion has turned golden, add the slices of farinheiras and let everything cook for 3 minutes, stirring from time to time.

Whisk the 6 eggs, then pour them into the pan and let them cook for a minute before stirring.

Season with salt and pepper to taste.

NB: don't forget the farinheiras are already pretty salty, of course!

Bom apetite!

At the heart of the country – inland Alentejo

Here we are in the middle of our journey south to the Algarve, after a first half that gave us a healthy dose of picturesque villages, scenery almost too spectacular to be real and intensely emotional experiences. Even once we'd passed the point where we thought the best was behind us!

But the programme for the next few days promises plenty of new surprises and unforgettable moments as Alentejo stretches out before us, with its wide range of artisanal traditions, its vineyards, its nature, its star-studded skies and much, much more.

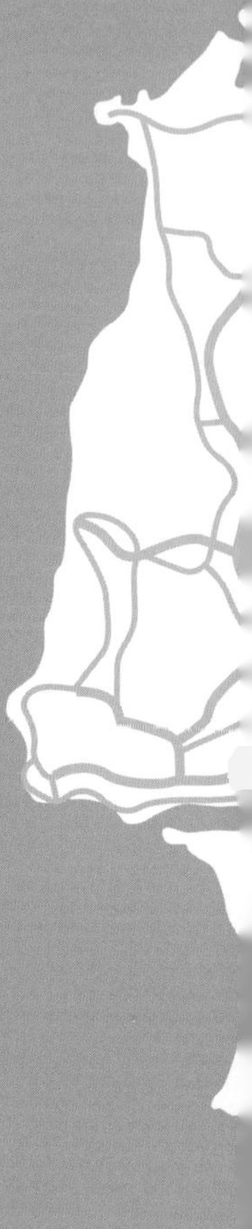

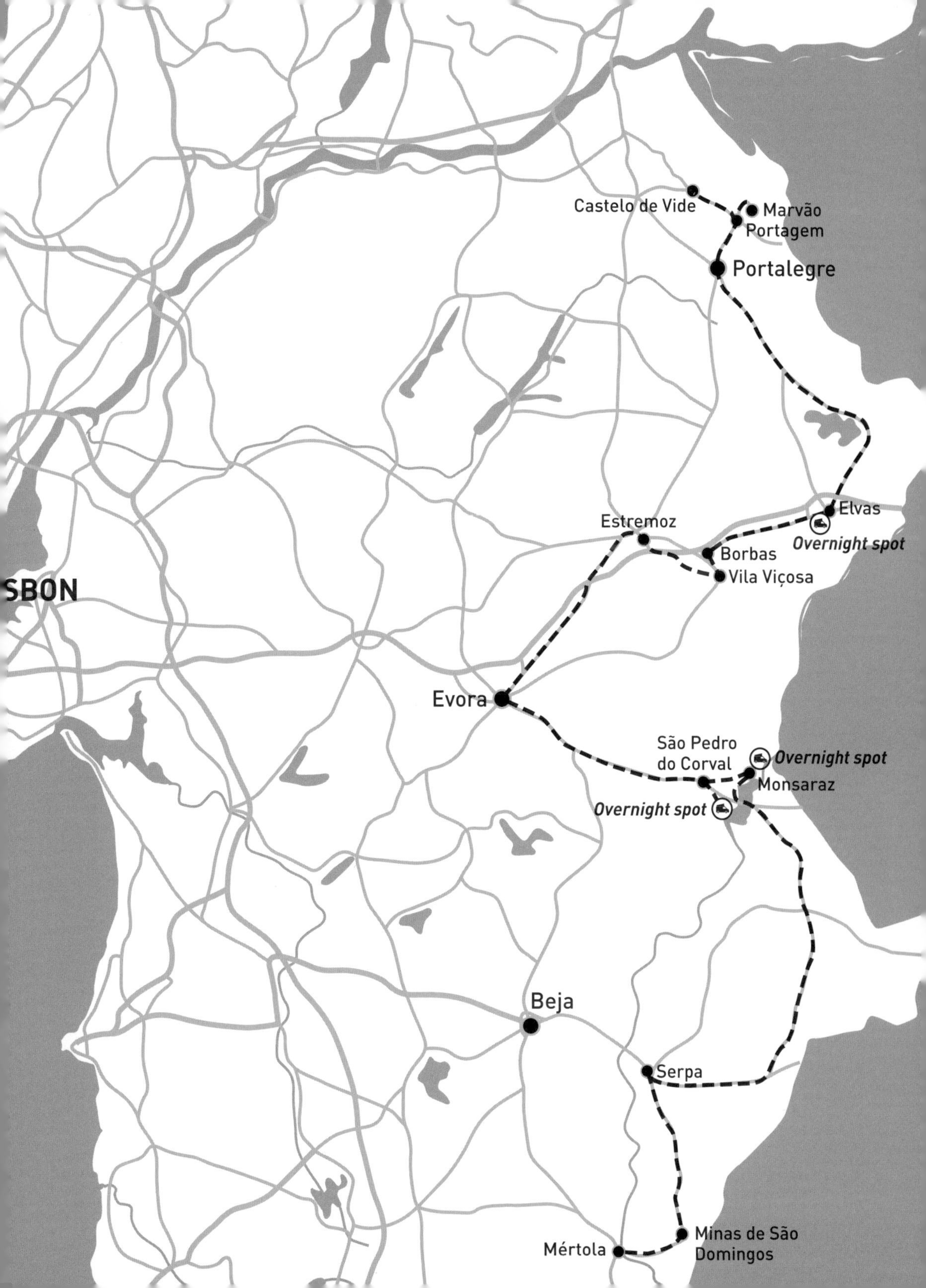
Castelo de Vide
Marvão
Portagem
Portalegre
Elvas
Overnight spot
Estremoz
Borbas
Vila Viçosa
SBON
Evora
São Pedro do Corval
Overnight spot
Monsaraz
Overnight spot
Beja
Serpa
Mértola
Minas de São Domingos

First steps in Alentejo

After nearly two weeks in Portugal, we now approach the town of Castelo de Vide, which marks our entry into Alto Alentejo, one of the four subareas into which Alentejo, Portugal's largest region, is divided. It's a large chunk, so we start with a visit to the Serra de São Mamede Natural Park, along the Spanish border.

Castelo de Vide is quite remarkable with its rich architecture, the white and yellow ochre facades that are typical of the region, its well preserved fortified centre and the peaceful atmosphere despite a certain morning bustle. This lovely town is brimming with places of interest, from the castle quarter to the Igreja Matriz de Santa Maria da Devesa square and numerous fountains. If you don't want to miss anything, your best bet is to do the PR5, a walk that takes you to all the sights and lets you explore the town thoroughly while refreshing yourself with crystal-clear water.

Our wheels now take us on to Marvão, a really cool fortified village, as we discover when we arrive. The castle at the top of the hill is magnificent, and the streets with their white houses are amazing too. Our advice in the October heat, still with temperatures of almost 30°C, is to sip a glass of something outside of *O Castelo* cafe and enjoy the view! Our second tip is to drive on to Portagem and relax at the Praia Fluvial, a stretch of the River Sever that has been turned into a municipal bathing area. The water must be about 10°C now that we're in October, but it undoubtedly gets warmer at other times! Whatever: a reviving dip never does any harm.

Next, we head for the town of Portalegre at the park exit. This is a fair-sized town, ideal for refuelling and stocking up on supplies. And it also offers a historical and artistic experience with a visit to the Museu da Tapeçaria Guy Fino, i.e. tapestry museum. It seems the town turned this craft into an art form in the mid-twentieth century.

The factory, which you can't visit, is still in business, with orders from the Portuguese State as well as many international artists. Next to the factory is the Robinson centre, which is housed in the former cork factory of the same name and the old convent of São Francisco dating back to the eighteenth century. The centre is part of a programme of conversion to new uses in the quarter. It is now a space for artistic and cultural associations and projects, while also allowing visitors to admire the old buildings.

We now leave the Serra de São Mamede and head for Elvas, blessed with the world's largest system of fortifications with ramparts and dry moats. It also has a massive aqueduct that reaches heights of more than 30 metres in places. We are now driving towards the famous marble towns of Vila Viçosa, Borba, Estremoz and Evora. The region is lucky enough to have deposits that are said to be sufficient for two centuries of quarrying. You can guess the decor in these towns: nearly all surfaces are clad in the famous stone. Old buildings, steps, paving – there's marble everywhere!

Incidentally, Evora is reckoned to be one of the country's most attractive towns. White dominates here too, including in the immaculate walls of the Igreja de São Francisco. If you are passing that way, the Capela dos Ossos close by is also worth a visit (5 euros per person, open all year round). It will undoubtedly make an impression: it is decorated entirely with bones taken from no fewer than 5,000 corpses in the region's cemeteries, in a morbid but spectacular allegory of the ephemeral nature of our existence. Evora also has plenty of great places where you can recover from the emotional impact of this chapel (see our recommended addresses).

Great addresses we found

Miradouro do Penedo Monteiro

39°25'11.7"N | 7°27'36.9"W

Car park for day and night, ideal for starting your visit to the citadel in good time and for drinking your fill at one of the town's many fountains.

Caballo Marvão

Abegões, caixa 14, Santo António das Areias, 7330-202 Portalegre

For horse riding in the heart of the Serra de São Mamede Natural Park.

Overnight spot

38°52'47.0"N | 7°10'32.5"W

Elvas

The closer you get to a large town, the more difficult it becomes to find a quiet place to spend the night. Elvas is no exception to this rule but never fear, we've found the solution!

You can park close to the funeral complex on a little-used road leading to its car park (a cul-de-sac in the form of a loop). Perched up on high and looking down on an olive grove, the spot is relatively quiet (we recommend parking in the middle of the loop on the small path leading to the stone gate). It also offers an unparalleled view of the ramparts and the town's historic aqueduct.

You see a thousand and one different things when you're on a camper van trip. Towns, monuments, scenery. You can also find your-

Under the stars of Alqueva

self in the middle of nowhere looking up at the sky. You can't fail to be moved by the beauty of a starry night. And who hasn't felt rather overwhelmed in the face of the vast night sky? Yet it's difficult to imagine taking your telescope with you when you're organizing your next road trip and packing the car, even if you're an amateur astronomer. But never mind, Dark Sky Alqueva is there to make up for your lack of equipment. Laymen as we are, we were unable to resist the call of interstellar space.

Armed with nothing more than our naked eyes but full of enthusiasm, we arrived at the Dark Sky Alqueva at nightfall, in the little village of Cumeada, deep in a rural area with very little light pollution. The team members, who include our hosts Rebecca (who specializes in ecotourism) and Nuno (an astronomer), work on a daily basis to keep it that way. The entire

region around Lake Alqueva (part of which is across the border in Spain) and its night skies are classified by UNESCO as a dark-sky destination for stargazing.

After a brief presentation in the observatory, housed in a former school, we find ourselves in the courtyard where space has been made for two telescopes (worth about 40,000 euros each). Despite the full moon and the presence of a few clouds, Nuno has no difficulty making it an exciting evening thanks to his expertise. He answers all our questions about the make-up of the constellations, their positions, how stars are born and so on. It's a fascinating immersion in the origins of our universe in a completely relaxed ambience.
Whether you are a keen stargazer or simply curious, we highly recommend contacting DSA for a stargazing session (€20 for adults, €10 for children aged 8–12, free for children under 8). Nuno and his colleagues will enjoy guiding you through the stars. The sky is open all year round, in the winter for a different perspective or in the summer for the best views of the Milky Way.

Finally, for anyone who did decide to take their telescope with them in their camper van, a free campsite is available a few minutes' drive from the observatory, on the banks of Lake Alqueva. From there, you can admire the celestial bodies without the slightest interference from light pollution, in peaceful surroundings. Truly off-grid.

Observatório Oficial Dark Sky Alqueva

R. da Nossa Sra. da Conceição 44,
7200-071 Cumeada

€20 for adults, €10 for children aged 8–12, free for children under 8.

Overnight spot

38°21'19.6"N | 7°26'38.1"W

Lake Alqueva

For anyone who did decide to take their telescope with them in their camper van, a free campsite is available a few minutes' drive from the observatory, on the banks of Lake Alqueva. From there, you can admire the stars in complete peace without any light pollution during the night, and make the most of the lake by getting out your SUP board or working on your breaststroke during the day. Or you could be like the locals, install yourself on the nearby bridge and get out your fishing rod!

DRIVE YOUR ADVENTURE

Clay soil

After a day spent sunning ourselves on the banks of Lake Alqueva, we get ready to continue our journey south. But first we make a detour to São Pedro do Corval. Situated right in the centre of the clay soil area of eastern Portugal, this small town is considered to be the national capital of pottery. And that in itself is enough to warrant a short visit.

With only a few thousand inhabitants and a population that is stagnating or even shrinking, like many other rural areas in Portugal, São Pedro do Corval is hardly a tourist hub. Far from it. But the town is surviving thanks to its twenty-two pottery workshops or *olarias*. These little family businesses are the pride of the region.
Pottery is also a key industry in Reguengos de Monsaraz and the surrounding area. The clay soil has in fact been exploited since prehistoric times. And as far as our hosts for today are concerned, for nearly a century.

The Olaria O Patalim was founded in 1927 and is still run by the same family, represented today by Nelia, who is kind enough to answer our questions in between brushstrokes. Because if you visit this *olaria*, not only will you be able to buy an attractive souvenir from among their huge collection of objects for the home (such as a little bowl designed for olives with a separate section for the pits for €4.50), you will also get a front-row seat from which to admire the skills of these craftsmen and craftswomen. The master potter works right in front of you while the painting, firing and varnishing take place a little further along. It's a small step, straight from the clay soil into your van.

Olaria O Patalim

São Pedro do Corval R. M514:
38°26'43.0"N | 7°28'53.6"W

To find more about the local craftsmanship in a family pottery workshop and (why not?) treat yourself to a small souvenir.

Switching to night mode

As the day comes to an end and your van is parked in the spot of your dreams, there is only one obstacle between you and complete relaxations: turning your van into its night-time configuration. Hardly an insurmountable obstacle, you will agree!

If you have a van with a push-up roof, all you have to do is unclip the roof, open a door, window or sunroof to let the air in, and push. There you have it: a height worthy of a chic apartment with removable mezzanine corner. Pure luxury!
In general, your van in day mode will have a very different arrangement to its setup in night mode. Unless you want to sleep on the little fold-away dining table, and that probably applies to only a small minority. Others will probably want to tidy things away when they go to sleep, a process that can be simplified by choosing to use the top bunk and reserving the 'ground floor' as storage space. If you feel you can't sleep at the top (freezing cold, strong winds, a desire for privacy), of course you will need to make space below.

Anyway, if you've parked far from any light pollution, as in Campinho, you will be able to open the windows, the sunroof or the skylight or even go outside to examine the night sky and the stars. Certain apps such as SkySafari, Star Walk 2 or Star Chart are very comprehensive and will help you identify what you see before you – and above you.

Overnight spot

38°26'33.2"N | 7°22'47.4"W

Under the ramparts of Monsaraz

It has been a packed day! A visit to an *olaria* in the morning, a visit to a *herdade* in the afternoon, an olive oil tasting session followed by wine tasting (see the next page) and we met Florian, a video maker who will be accompanying us for the next two days.

We've been so busy that we weren't able to get to our next planned stop south of the Vale do Guadiana Natural Park. But no problem: we might not have time but we're pretty resourceful! As the day comes to an end, we stop in one of the amazing paved parking areas built as terraces at the foot of the ramparts of Monsaraz. They are well arranged and offer awesome views of the surroundings. What more could you want?

But we get more anyway. The little village of Monsaraz is totally charming and although many restaurants are closed at this time of year, we do get a warm welcome at restaurant *O Gaspacho*. Local wines and delicious *petiscos* prepared by the authentically gruff chef of the establishment. All you need for a successful evening.

Walls - Mogli

A story of oil and wine

It all started long before our trip when we sent an e-mail to Carmim, a cooperative for the production of olive oil in the area Reguengos de Monsaraz. We didn't get a reply but, stubborn as we are, we decide to drop in on them anyway. Unfortunately, no one is available to talk to us. Nevertheless, a nice young guy in charge of sales gives us the address of a local producer and off we set for Herdade do Esporão.

When we arrive, to our surprise it is nothing like the little outfit we had been expecting! Herdade do Esporão, officially founded in 1267, is a huge estate covering 1,834 hectares including an artificial lake created in 1985. It also owns various properties in the Portalegre and Douro regions. The restaurant, the wine bar – everything is beautifully designed. To be honest, we feel a tiny bit out of place in such sophisticated surroundings.

That feeling lasts about fifteen seconds, until we are met in the lobby. We are swiftly led to the wine bar for an olive oil tasting session. Now we can get down to the serious business. Six different oils, ranging from the very mild to the very strong (Selecção, an amazing oil) and all absolutely delicious and a delight for the palate, accompanied by bread made on the estate. There's nothing like it for building up strength for the main challenge.

Because Luis now takes charge of us for a private tour of the estate, from the vineyards to the cellar. Our guide knows his subject like the back of his hand, from the rich history of the place to how each vintage is bottled. We learn for example that in 2007 the estate started a switch to 100 per cent certified organic production, which it has now completed. It uses only natural processes to combat parasites, following the introduction of cultivation helpmates such as ladybirds or bats and planting suitable plants (rosebushes, rosemary) to make them feel at home.

Luis also goes into detail of the actual production: 1 million litres of olive oil a year and 14 million litres of wine (75 per cent red wine, 25 per cent white). Despite such huge volumes, they respect the traditional methods. They even have a wine, the *vinho de talha*, based on a technique used back in the Roman Empire: it is kept in large clay amphora, the inside of which is covered with a mix of beeswax, olive oil and pine resin. For the more traditional production, they use 2,500 oak barrels from America and France, which do their job in the shadows 17 metres underground while 300,000 bottles also wait to reach the right age. A well-oiled process from start to finish.

Herdade do Esporão

Apartado 31,
7200-999 Reguengos de Monsaraz

Whether you are looking for a good meal, an olive oil tasting (€7 per person) or a wine tasting. If you want to roll up your sleeves, you can even pay a visit during the grape harvest (mid-August to end of September) and pick some grapes before a visit plus a tasting and a meal. Reservation required. www.esporao.com

Vale do Guadiana Natural Park

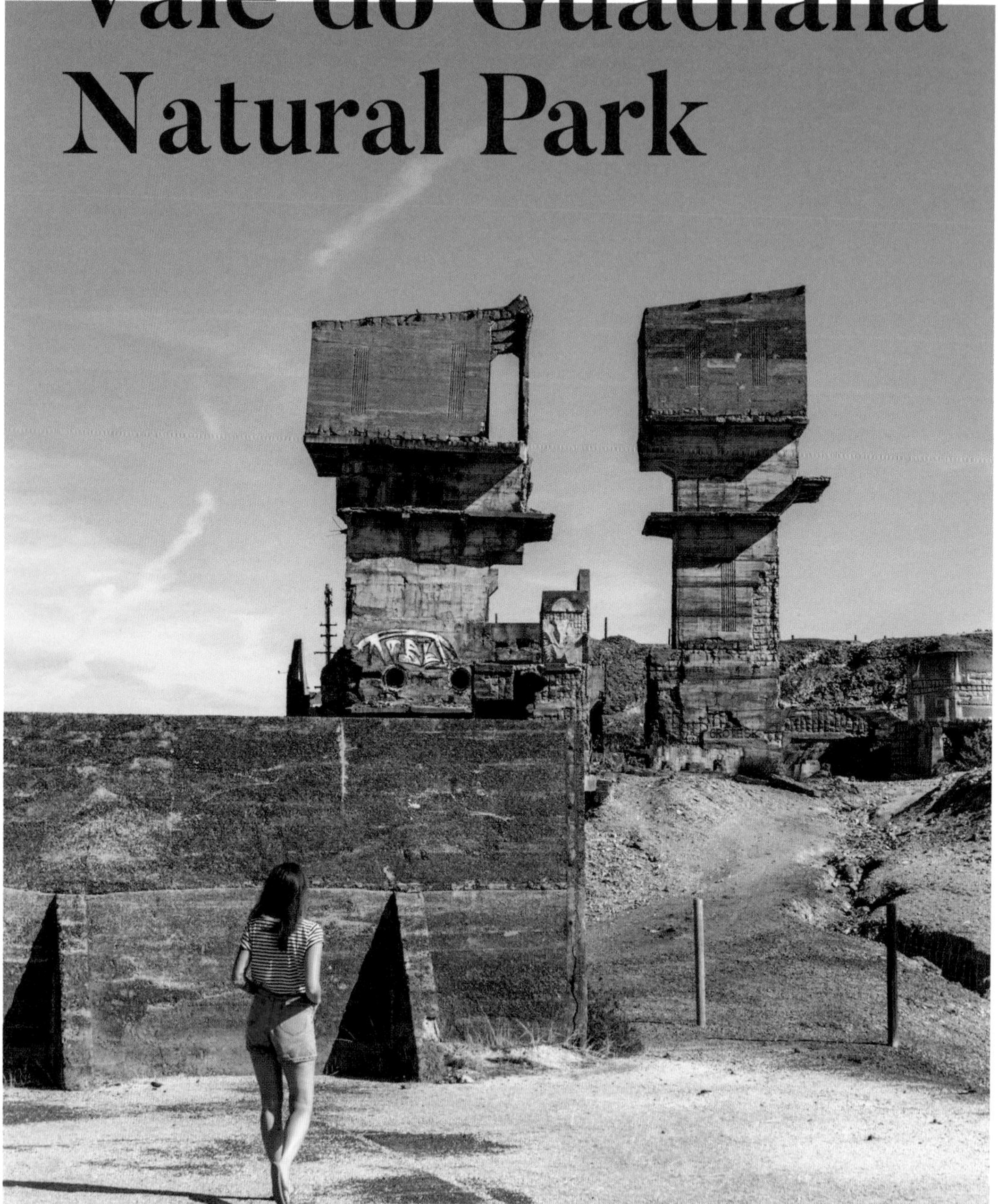

The further south we get and the closer to the coast, the more we see the scenery changing. After crossing relatively arid countryside in the north of the country, we now see land that is almost desert-like through our windows. It should be said Portugal had been experiencing an unusually dry period for weeks at this point. We now arrive in the Vale do Guadiana Natural Park, appropriately named as the eponymous river crosses it from north to south. Somewhere to cool down that will be very welcome if you visit the park in the summer, given that the highest temperatures ever recorded in Portugal were measured here.

The temperature in mid-October is quite pleasant, however. Anyway, to stay in dry mode and explore some industrial archaeology, we decide to visit the abandoned mines of Mina de São Domingos. This ancient complex for excavating copper and sulphur, where mining first took place in Roman times and restarted in the nineteenth century and closed again in 1966, can be reached by a very manageable dirt track. Witness to a bygone age, the dilapidated site is a dramatic setting. However, we wouldn't recommend bathing in its waters as they are not exactly crystal clear...

The town of Mina de São Domingos has had trouble surviving the loss of its mining industry. In the absence of other activities, it seems to live in slow motion nowadays. You can still enjoy its river-bank beach (praia fluvial) where there is a large rest area equipped for camper vans and RVs. Staying with the history theme, you can also take a look (free of charge) at the Casa do Mineiro where an old miner's home has been reconstructed.
Next, we drive on to the little town of Mértola. While it has a certain charm, located on the west bank of the river and with a castle perched on the hill, it is primarily an excellent base thanks to its position in the middle of the park. From here it takes quarter of an hour, largely on a dirt track, to get to Moinho do Canais, a great spot for bathing located at a dead end, deep in a canyon. We advise you to get there early, though, as there are only two parking spaces!

Finally, we return to Mértola to end the day in a beautiful setting and regain our strength by treating ourselves to a meal in restaurant Terra Utopica.

Guadiana from a different perspective

You are free to plunge point-blank into your visit to Vale do Guadiana Natural Park. After all, these parks are free spaces that you can explore at your own pace. However, if you're short of inspiration for what to see or do while in the park, you don't need to look any further!

Take a trip to the little town of Serpa. If you have a large van or motorhome, park it outside the town walls as entry is restricted to vehicles 2 m in width (and it only takes a few minutes to walk to the centre). Drop in at the small cafe *Serpa Lovers*. Not only will you be able to enjoy a refreshing beverage and one of their delicious pastries, but Vera, the owner of the place, will also be delighted to tell you about the various organizations that can liven up your visit to the park.
One of Vera's partners is Pure Land, for instance. Based south of Mértola, this little company offers a whole range of activities in the Guadiana valley, such as excursions in a 4x4 or on mountain bikes, stand-up paddling, an introduction to abseiling, ziplining (up to 150 m), birdwatching or paintballing in the abandoned ruins of Mina de São Domingos!

Serpa Lovers also has an assortment of natural beauty products (soaps, essential oils etc.), produced locally by Herdade de Vale Côvo, which is located not far from the Guadiana River in the middle of the park. If you're looking to spend a peaceful night surrounded by nature, this place can also point you to agritourist accommodation.

Great addresses we found

Restaurant Terra Utopica

R. Dom Sancho II 41, 7750-350 Mértola

We were taken immediately by its peaceful outdoor seating area with views down onto the river, and we were totally won over by the Porco Preto (an Iberian pork dish typical of the south of the peninsula), which was absolutely delicious. At €13, the *plumas* are out of this world. A tip for fans!

Caféteria Guadiana

R. 25 de Abril 2, 7750-332 Mértola

For a cup of coffee, a pastry, a snack or a quick lunch. In our case, we settled down inside to enjoy a cheese and cold meat platter and take advantage of the sockets and Wi-Fi!

Heading south

After slightly more than two weeks travelling and exploring, we have nearly finished crossing Portugal from north to south. This route has let us get to know parts of the country that are off the beaten tourist track but rich in history and nature.

Now we are leaving the Portuguese interior and driving to the coast, to areas that have largely been transformed by and for tourism. And although we shudder at the thought of the inherent urbanization associated with all that, we're still looking forward to the Atlantic coast and tracking down places that have retained their original charm. In other words, discovering the Portugal of your dreams: sand, sun, surfers chasing the perfect wave...

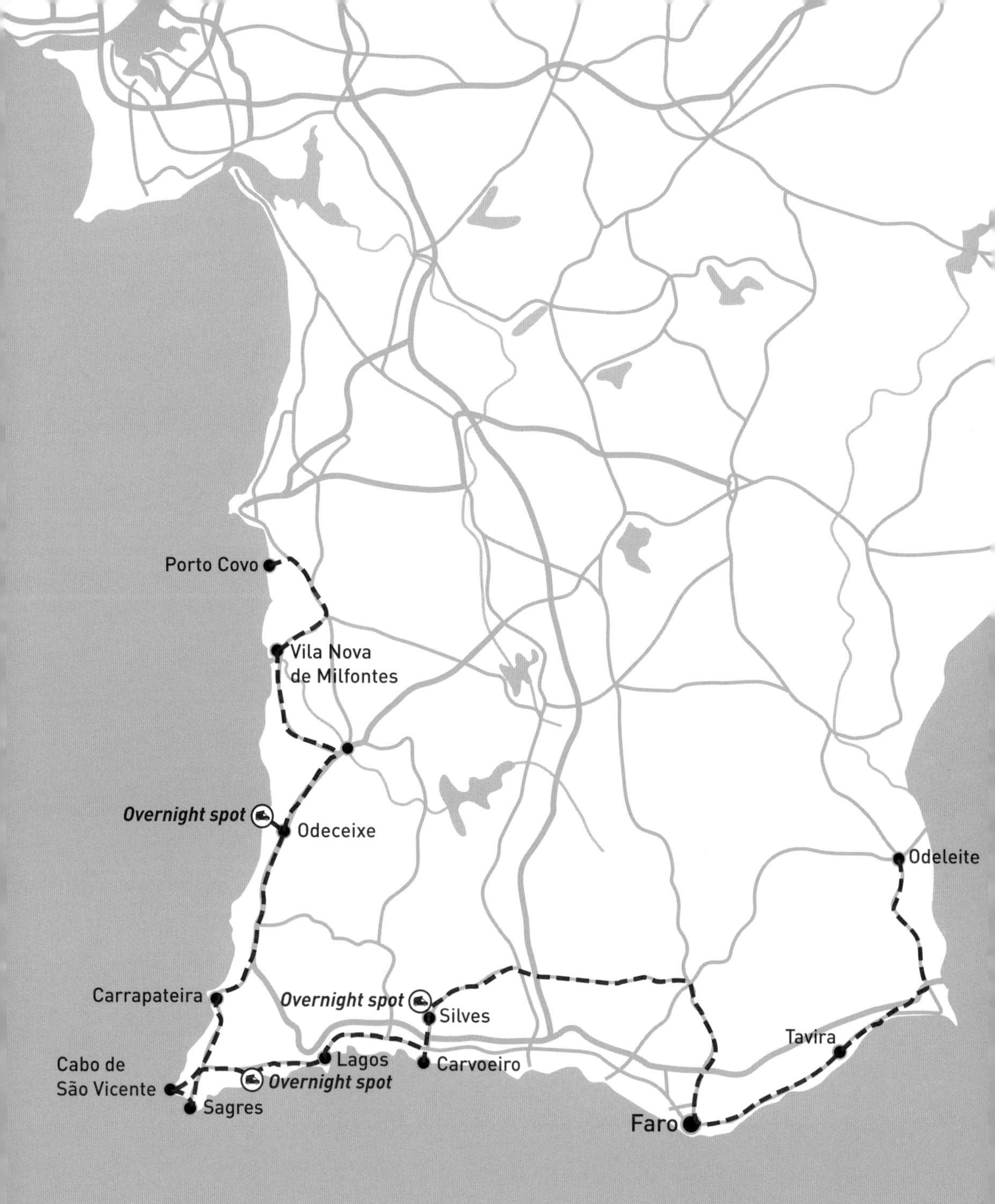
Porto Covo
Vila Nova
de Milfontes
Overnight spot
Odeceixe
Odeleite
Carrapateira
Overnight spot
Silves
Tavira
Cabo de
São Vicente
Lagos
Carvoeiro
Overnight spot
Sagres
Faro

The home of the Blue Dragon

Goodbye Alentejo, hello Algarve! It's time to head for the far south of Portugal. We leave Mértola in the late morning aiming to reach the south Atlantic coast in one go, while allowing ourselves the option of one or two detours.

It doesn't take long for the opportunity to arise! As we drive along the IC27, a large lake on the right catches our eye. We are soon persuaded by its intense blue so we take the next exit and set off in that direction. A dirt and pebble track takes us to the banks of the lake, which was created when the Odeleite dam was built. It is actually the river of the same name that we are looking at. It is also called the Blue Dragon as it resembles that Chinese character when seen from the air (look it up on the net to get an idea of what we're talking about!).

Anyway, what's most important to us is that the rather bumpy track eventually gets us to a wide beach in greens and yellows, further enriching the colourful scene of the lake's waters (37°19'52.5"N | 7°30'36.0"W). It's the perfect spot for an afternoon swim, taking the SUP board out or simply relaxing in the sun. We only had a brief stop but we highly recommend the detour. The road might seem rather challenging but you'll get there in the end.

♫ A Way of Life - Hans Zimmer

Day-to-day logistics in a camper van

As setting up camp is not allowed except at certain RV parking areas or at campsites, local municipalities often provide plenty of facilities and service areas to compensate for this ban and avoid you having to go to a campsite to perform minor everyday tasks.

Where can you do your clothes washing? In the case of Portugal, we now know you should go to a shopping mall or an Intermarché car park! They have launderettes with washing machines (8 and 18 kg) and tumble-dryers (18 kg) that are usually open twenty-four hours. Reckon on about 4 euros for the small washing machine, 8 euros for the large one and 2 euros for 20 minutes drying.

Where can you get fresh supplies of water? In some service areas for RVs (next to the disposal points for blackwater waste) or service stations. This might be your most complicated task in Portugal, especially because the locals don't drink tap water. If in doubt, ask whether the service is freely available and the water safe to drink. Most service stations have a hose you can use at the same place where you can pump up your tyres. This service might be free of charge but we'd suggest combining it with refuelling to thank them and encourage such generous services! Allow some time too as the flow can be pretty feeble.

Where can you empty your water tank and/or your chemical toilet? These are facilities you can find easily pretty much everywhere. You will also often find them in combination in the same place: in the municipal service areas (more or less routinely), in RV parking areas, at certain supermarket car parks, at service stations or at the entrance to municipal campsites, for instance. While access to drains for emptying your water tank is usually free of charge, you will have to pay to empty your toilet wastewater (chemical toilet). Reckon on 2 to 3 euros.

The Ria Formosa, jewel of the Algarve

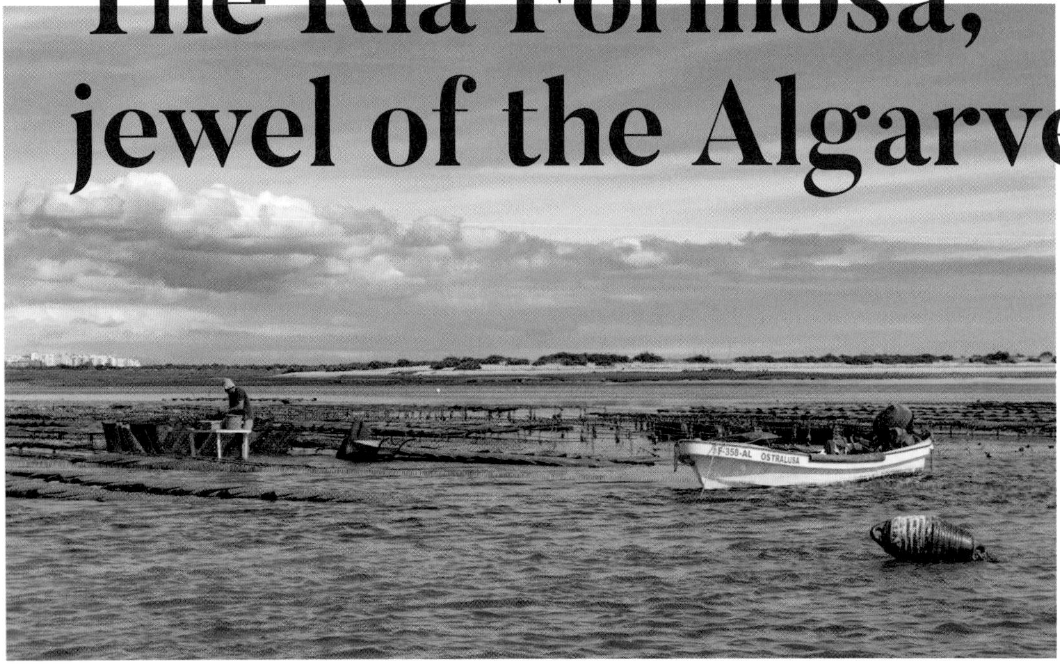

Portugal has been our temporary home for less than three weeks and we are already on the southern Atlantic coast. This part of the country is rather less wild-looking, as the urbanization of the coast has done its job, but there's one area that is almost untouched: the Ria Formosa Natural Park. Ria means 'estuary' (even if that's not actually the case here as it's more of a lagoon) and Formosa is an old-fashioned word to describe a woman with shapely curves. In other words, just the park's name will give you plenty to discuss...

We arrive in the protected area near Tavira. Although the park is centred on the country's southernmost point, it actually stretches almost 60 kilometres from east to west, covering an area of 18,400 hectares. Its eastern section mainly consists of beaches, some of which are (for our taste) a tad over-managed and overrun by bars and restaurants. Nature lovers, for example, will do well to avoid the beaches of Ilha de Tavira and will probably prefer the Praia do Barril. You can get to that beach by a small train (1.6 euros per person), with reasonably priced parking available at the departure station. When you get there, you will find some restaurants, stone-built rather than made of plastic, and an anchor cemetery giving the place a certain charm.

The real highlight is to be found further west, next to Faro. Here, the lagoon changes appearance depending on the tides, which can vary the sea level by as much as 4 metres! To experience this from close up, we get in contact with Natura Algarve, which offers boat trips for spotting the local wildlife, among other things. By wildlife we mainly mean birds, but there are also fiddler crabs and, if you're

very lucky, otters (best to go at the end of the day for them) and dolphins.

The Ria Formosa was made a protected zone and nature reserve in 1978 and became an official natural park in 1987; it is now a sanctuary for many species of birds, both resident and migratory, and of fish. Fishing in the lagoon is restricted and subject to regulations. The lagoon is also used for oyster farms, clam farms (80 per cent of Portugal's total production) and salt extraction.

Great addresses we found

Natura Algarve

Avenida da República - Stand 2, Doca de Recreio de Faro, 8000-078 Faro

This little ecotourism company offers boat trips in the heart of the Ria Formosa with various themes: a comprehensive tour of the park, birdwatching, dolphin spotting, customized private boat trips etc. The birdwatching excursion of 2½ hours with a biologist costs €35 per person (€17 for children under 10).

The Serra do Caldeirão

You may have noticed that we are not great fans of places that bear the stamp of mass tourism. While we don't want to avoid the coast entirely, we prefer to bypass areas that are particularly crowded or have been built up beyond all recognition.

After our first stint on Portugal's south coast, it's therefore only natural that we decide to move inland again to explore the Serra do Caldeirão ('cauldron mountain range' in English), which forms a natural border in the east between the Algarve and Alentejo. After a rainy Saturday spent waiting in a charming car park in the little village of Querença, we set off for Rocha da Pena where we plan to walk the trail of the same name the next day. Note that the road from Querença to Alte is also very scenic.

We set off at eight on Sunday morning from where we parked for the night, just a few metres from where the trail starts. (If you can talk about a start to a trail that is basically a loop.) The best option is to choose Rocha for its little cafe on the side of the road, especially during the summer when temperatures on the plateau can get sweltering. A refreshing stop when you get there will be very welcome.

The loop took us a good two hours to complete, going at a relaxed pace with plenty of time for photos and admiring the amazing scenery in the morning sun. Plus an unexpected short shower as we were descending. Taken as a whole, the Rocha da Pena trail is not at all difficult with a climb of 285 m over a distance of 6.7 km. An excellent walk to stretch your legs.

Overnight spot

37°11'14.7"N | 8°27'04.9"W

Algarve Motorhome Park Silves

All experts will tell you that two things are essential after a morning of physical activity. The first is to take a shower and enjoy the soothing sensation as you spread your toes! The second is to top up your glucose levels. By which we mean treating yourself to something sweet because you deserve it.
In the interests of efficiency and to get those two crucial tasks done, we have parked at the Silves motorhome campsite, next to the N124 and a stone's throw from a hypermarket (8.5 euros for 24 hours, with electricity). We're obviously not talking an idyllic spot. But it is peaceful and has everything you need (electricity, Wi-Fi, showers, place to dispose of wastewater, boules pitch). Or almost. If you want the toilet, you have to go to the supermarket 200 metres away, but this is also an opportunity to buy the ingredients for our delicious almond gateau, for example. You need that sugar, remember! (See p. 107)

♫ *It Ain't Me Babe - Joaquin Phoenix and Reese Witherspoon*

The Seven Hanging Valleys

When you read and hear about Portugal, you are often told that the Algarve is the ultimate must-see region. To check whether it deserves that reputation, we decide to go on one of the must-do trips in this must-see region: the Seven Hanging Valleys trail. A kind of 'must' squared.

We leave Fernão, fiercely guarded by our cat Nel, in the shade on the side of the access road to the Praia do Vale de Centeanes (37°05'29.0"N | 8°27'14.8"W), the point of departure for the Seven Hanging Valleys trail.
Our advice is to arrive early in the morning in order to be sure of getting a free parking space in the dead-end road leading to the beach. The route starts with wooden steps marked by the familiar red and yellow strips. Off we go!

While some stretches are a little trickier than our previous hiking outing, this trail is not any more physically demanding. The 5.7 kilometres take us to the top of sheer cliffs with the ocean tens of metres below, winding along rock formations and descending to secluded beaches before climbing up again. It's a pleasant trail that lets you admire the stunning landscape along the route, doable in two hours at a leisurely pace. Allow twice that if you want to stop for views and a couple of swims. Definitely a must-do!
Some points to note for people without much hiking experience:

- While it's not particularly dangerous, some stretches do need the appropriate gear, at the very least proper walking shoes.

Darlin' Do Not Fear - Brett Dennen

• The trail goes in a straight line from Praia do Vale de Centeanes to Praia da Marinha (or vice versa). So if, like us, you prefer to go one way only, you will have to arrange a means of transport to get back to the start of your walk.

• For that reason, we recommend choosing Praia da Marinha as your destination (37°05'24.4"N | 8°24'45.0"W) as you will find it easier to hitch-hike back from there (thanks to our Australian friends Mandy and Bernie for picking us up!) or order a taxi (reckon on about 15 euros) at the kiosks next to the car park.

• You can extend the hike by about two kilometres by starting from the awesome Algar Seco site. There is also parking available there (37°05'35.6"N | 8°27'55.1"W).

• It's easy to lose the trail at the Praia de Benagil. To find it again, climb back up to the *O Algar* restaurant and turn right between the restaurant and its little car park, where you will see a red and yellow painted sign on the rock face.

• It's a good idea to leave very early in the morning when the trail is still quiet, especially in summer if you also want to avoid the sweltering heat. Some parts of the route double up as access to beaches and so those sections start to get very busy by the end of the morning. If you're a keen photographer, that is also the time of day when the light is at its most golden.

Great addresses we found

Boneca Bar

Estr. do Algar Seco, 8400-531 Carvoeiro

Under one of the lovely awnings that elegantly screen the outdoor seating, nestled among the rocks of Algar Seco.

Almond gateau

Ingredients for 4 people

3 eggs

100 g muscovado sugar (brown sugar)

125 g ground almonds

150 g flour

125 g softened or melted butter

lemon zest (or lemon extract)

a handful of chopped almonds

Preparation

Beat the eggs with the sugar.

Add the flour, then the ground almonds.

Mix in the melted butter and the lemon.

Butter the ovenproof silicone mould.

Sprinkle some chopped almonds onto the base of the mould.

Pour the dough into the mould, then add some more chopped almonds on top.

Cooking

Put the gateau in the oven and place it on the stove for about 20 minutes, checking from time to time. When the gateau looks sufficiently golden, test it's cooked through with the blade of a knife.

Enjoy this gateau at any time of the day, preferably while warm, on its own or with a spread. (No palm oil!)

Nowhere2Far Sunrise Tour

To visit the Algarve and not admire the caves of Ponta da Piedade would undoubtedly be a gross mistake. The famous headland two kilometres south of Lagos is one of those famous must-sees. Although you can get to it on foot, the best impression of the caves in all their glory is from the ocean, especially at sunrise. That's enough to persuade us to meet up with Holly and David, the founders of Nowhere2far. Specialized in paddle boarding adventures, they are the only organization to offer trips early in the morning before the coast is invaded by tourist groups and fishermen in motorboats. This Englishwoman from Cornwall and her Australian boyfriend probably never ought to have met. We'll give you the short version!

It's 2007 and Holly and David both have work that takes them around the world: she is a member of a competitive yachting team and he is the chief mechanic on a pleasure boat. When the twists and turns of fate disrupted their dreams, the paths of the former wannabe climbing instructor and the high jumper who'd abandoned hopes of the Olympics due to injury crossed when they both docked at Genoa. It was love at first sight. After several years of adventures together, including cycling from England to Australia, they settled in Portugal and started their business in 2018. The sequel is still being written!

Which brings us back to Praia da Dona Ana where we meet David at seven in the morning, just before sunrise. Despite a doubtful weather forecast causing a delay to our departure, we slip into our wetsuits and start paddling. And we're off, for a three-hour trip (50 euros per person) along the coast and past the caves to discover spots that can only be reached by using your arm muscles. The whole experience is unique and incredible, while David's upbeat attitude is bound to put a smile on your face.

When we get back to our starting point, David and Holly (who joins us with their little daughter Anissa, aged two) get out the thermos flasks to offer the group coffee and biscuits. It's a long, lovely moment to share with one another and get our breath back before changing, chatting and rinsing off at the back of Fernão (you can take your time as no one will rush you!). One hour later, all five of us (Nel is still sleeping) repair to *Twin Fin* cafe to carry on chatting and enjoy a delicious brunch. David and Holly are fascinating to listen to and won't fail to entertain you with the long version of their adventures. If you're anything like us, you'll find it hard to say goodbye!

New Light - John Mayer

Great addresses we found

Nowhere2Far Stand-up paddle

Alameda Dr. Armando Soares Ribeiro, 8600-315 Lagos

Meeting point and start of the Sunrise Tour. The spaces at the lower end of the car park are relatively flat so you can park your van there the night before to make sure you're on time for the very early meet-up the next day!

Twin Fin

R. Gil Vicente 32, 8600-596 Lagos

Surf Café. The perfect address for sharing a brunch after a trip in the sea off Lagos. The hot drinks are delicious (which isn't always the case in Portugal). On the menu, in addition to a traditional English breakfast, are avocado on toast, waffles with Iberian ham or with salmon, burgers with Australian sauce, a 'power bowl' and so on. Reckon on €10 to 15 per person (drink + 1 dish).

Overnight spot

37°04'20.0"N | 8°46'25.5"W

Burgau

Impeccable guides to the last, Holly and David point us to a car park where you can stay the night, overlooking the beach in the little town of Burgau. It's the perfect spot for a night lulled by the relaxing sound of the waves! The parking area is on the side of a very quiet road; it's peaceful and flat, with magnificent views. It also boasts public toilets complete with showers (cold) and is next to a cute little bar with excellent cocktails. You can also get to the town centre in no time, where you will find some good restaurants, in particular the pizzerias *Corso* and *Casa Padaria*. This is a small harbour town that has kept its authentic, natural character in the heart of the Algarve.

Mar Ilimitado

As the locals will tell you and as we can verify every day, the further west you get along the southern Atlantic coast, the wilder the scenery gets. And the more we feel the pull of the ocean. We were not lucky enough to see any dolphins when we went stand-up paddle boarding, so now we contact Mar Ilimitado, based in Sagres.

No catering for mass tourism here! That's for the simple and excellent reason that Mar Ilimitado was founded by biologists, is owned by biologists and (except for two boat skippers) only employs biologists. As Sara, one of the founders, explains to us, the organization's primary objective isn't actually tourism at all: it was set up in 2005 to tackle the lack of data about local marine wildlife. In particular, they wanted to learn more about cetaceans (whales and dolphins), many of which live in or visit the waters south of Sagres.

Biology as the goal and tourism as the means, you could say, as the guided excursions are used to finance the research carried out by this independent organization, which has three to eight employees depending on the season. Of the 'part-time' biologists, it's Ana (specialized in marine ecology) who informs us about the marine species that we are likely to see now, in late October, while also reminding us of the many environmental problems being inflicted upon the oceans. "We aren't asking anyone to be perfect, but everyone is capable of doing better by changing a few habits," she explains.

Next, we set off on a boat trip lasting 1½ hours (40 euros, 35 euros for a faster but less comfortable boat, 25 euros for children under 14) in the hope of seeing some dolphins (common or bottlenose). According to Ana, the chance of seeing at least one species of cetacean on a trip is at least 95 per cent – and we are inclined to believe her as we are soon surrounded by about fifty dolphins! It's an amazing experience and we are able to admire these gracious mammals swimming in front of our craft for nearly thirty minutes in the radiant sun.

Note that the aforementioned two species of dolphin can be spotted off the coast of the Algarve all year round. Some species of whale visit these waters at the start and end of the summer, while killer whales can occasionally be seen between June and September when these crafty dolphins (yes, it's a big family) follow the tuna passing Gibraltar to reproduce in the Mediterranean.

Mar Ilimitado

Porto da Baleeira de Sagres,
8650-368 Sagres

The Light - The Album Leaf

Hikes through history

There's nothing quite like a camper van road trip for letting you enjoy your favourite outdoor activities, especially when driving through a country like Portugal where you can surf in the morning and go horse riding in the afternoon. And where you sometimes only have to drive for a few minutes to get from the coastal paths to the mountain trails. In fact, you are never far from a hiking trail in this country. That is particularly so in the south, where two associations have a huge job mapping, surveying and maintaining these routes.

The first is Via Algarviana, which gets its name from the ancient pilgrim route crossing the Algarve from the banks of the Guadiana River in the east to the Sagres headland in the west. The route covers no less than 300 kilometres from its start on the Spanish border to the finish at Cabo de São Vicente in the southwest. The trail is designed to take in all the historical, natural and cultural sites of interest dotted along the route, as well as restaurants and other hospitality venues.

If you are not able to do the entire route, you can (of course) drive to various points in the route and just walk the sections you want depending on the themes that appeal most to you. All the necessary information about this fantastic route can be found at the site viaalgarviana.org.

The second association is called Rota Vicentina. While much of its work undoubtedly consists of maintenance, it is primarily the association's tool that makes it so popular with travellers. By 'tool' we mean the absolutely marvellous website rotavicentina.com, especially the interactive map. It lets you customize and modify your route (on foot or by bike) depending on your preferences.

It has an overview of possible trails with a filter option so that you can just see those that interest you, with one-way routes, loops, hiking-only or biking-only trails, themed routes such as the Fishermen's Trail, restaurants, accommodation and activities. In short, the Rota Vicentina website is the perfect tool for creating your personalized trail in the Sudoeste Alentejano e Costa Vicentina Natural Park. The website is available in Portuguese, English, French and German!

A route between land and sea

It's now almost four weeks since we arrived in Portugal, which means we are close to halfway through our trip. That shows we're on schedule: we entered the country in the northeast and here we are in the southwest. To start the day properly, we are therefore going to visit Portugal's bottom left corner, the Cabo de São Vicente, which also happens to be continental Europe's lowermost left corner. Note that you are not allowed to park for the night there. In fact, there's nothing charming about the place anyway with its numerous snack shacks and souvenir kiosks. It is also inundated by hordes of camper vans from sunrise to sunset.

Once we've paid this symbolic visit, we have the prospect of a scenic drive through the Pontal da Carrapateira (note that the association Rota Vicentina (see the preceding page) offers a signposted hiking trail along the same route). The route starts with the intriguing Museu do Mar e da Terra da Carrapateira, which has a collection of objects donated by local inhabitants that give you an insight into the history, habits and customs of this stretch of the coast. From this point on, the paved road becomes a dirt track and hugs the coast between Praia do Amado and Praia da Bordeira, in the Sudoeste Alentejano e Costa Vicentina Natural Park.

It's more of an outdoor museum than an ordinary route: intelligently designed with two large car parks, marked by asterisks on the map, one at either end, from where you can set off on a hiking adventure or explore the place by mountain bike (available on site). As you drive along, you will see numerous wooden footbridges nicely integrated into the surrounding landscape. They lead to lookout points giving amazing views of the ocean and the cliffs, and letting you spot sites such as the old Porto da Zimbreirinha where fishermen have braved the elements for more than a century, discover the ruins of a Moorish village dating back to the twelfth century or watch the surfers riding the waves. There are eleven access points in total, marked by two-metre-high letters in weathering steel running from A to K.

The beaches of Amado and Bordeira are the two places most favoured by surfers. Veteran surfers will undoubtedly be in their element while novices can get help from one of the surfing schools plying their wares all along the inviting stretch of white sand.

We are now right in the heart of a natural park, which means that camping and overnight parking are banned, but it looks as if wild camping is condoned out of season if the dozens of camper vans and motorhomes stationed in the various car parks are anything to go by. If you do decide to spend the night here, of course you should respect the environment and be discreet.

Times Like This - Jet

Praia da Fateixa

37°20'02.9"N | 8°51'32.9"W

Anyone taking the route between Amado and Bordeira or visiting the beach of Monte Clerigo will undoubtedly discover that these places are overwhelmed during the day. The same often applies at night, despite the strict ban on overnight stays along this section of the coastline.
But there's a solution for the daytime problem at any rate that will let you find quieter beaches not very far away with an effort that is not particularly physically demanding. Time to find the peace and quiet of Praia da Fateixa! You will find a number of parking spaces overlooking the beach, letting you leave your van perched a few dozen metres above the Atlantic. Ideal for an afternoon spent lazing around, swimming or surfing.

Where to wash when travelling by van in Portugal

It goes without saying but we'll say it anyway: having a shower in the back of your van definitely falls in the 'camping practices' category, especially if you plan on using a foldaway shower cubicle.

That means you will be obliged to use a water supply point separate from your vehicle for washing. Fortunately there are plenty of these tap points in Portugal, especially along the coast where the beaches often have (cold) showers.

If you want a slightly more comfortable wash, the options are service stations, public toilets (the ones near the coast often have showers too), municipal swimming baths and of course campsites.

Note that if you want to rinse off quickly after a day at the beach, no one will complain about you using your vehicle's outdoor shower hose!

Overnight spot

37°26'31.4"N | 8°47'42.1"W

Odeceixe

No need to be embarrassed: we don't know how to pronounce this name either. But we're mentioning it for another reason, namely because this little car park at the end of the route next to the mouth of the Ribeira de Seixe is such a quiet spot. A place where all the family will find something to amuse them!

The car park is located in the final bend of this little river, on the opposite bank to the village. It leads to the river bank beach, which you have to cross to get to the proper beach. So you can take your SUP board out onto the river, followed by a surfing session on the rolling waves of the Atlantic Ocean. Total length of the route: 200 metres. Who says the easy-to-reach options are inevitably the busiest?

Hiking fans will also be happy here as the car park is the perfect starting point for various trails – see the excellent Rota Vicentina website for details.
Finally, if that is what you fancy, there are some restaurants and bars only a few minutes' walk away, located a few dozen metres above the beach.

Olalla - Blanco White

The Fishermen's Trail

A highlight on Rota Vicentina's menu is the Trilho dos Pescadores, known as the Fishermen's Trail in English, a trail along the coast of Portugal from Lagos to Sines (226.5 kilometres). If you don't have time to walk the entire route, that's not a problem as numerous points are accessible by camper van.

In particular, there is the small town of Porto Covo, considered to be the final stage on the Vicentine coast. It's very quiet now in October, all the more so as the weather gods have not exactly smiled on us these past few days. Among the many restaurants on the main street, we come across the perfect place for a break: *Marquês – Cervejaria e Marisqueira*. It's a small, friendly cafe where you can enjoy pastries, hot dishes and ice creams in a charming setting. Just south of the town, the Praia do Sissal offers awesome views in this autumnal atmosphere, and a circular trail that you can do on foot, by bike or on horseback!

Indeed, if you want to spend more time in the northern part of the Sudoeste Alentejano e Costa Vicentina Natural Park, we have some tips for livening up your stay with some equestrian excursions! The Herdade do Pessegueiro, a quarter of an hour's drive south of Porto Covo, is just the thing for you.

We are familiar with the *herdades* ('farms') that specialize in producing wine or olive oil. Well, this farm specializes in horses. More specifically, horse breeding until recently and horses for tourism nowadays. Founded in 1986, the place exudes peace and tranquillity, as demonstrated by Beatriz who greets us when we arrive.

Of course you don't have to go horse riding. You could also rent one of the farm's six cottages to recharge your batteries.

The small scale of this *herdade* gives it a calm ambience. With three year-round employees, 35 horses of which 19 are available for excursions, nine hectares and a small artificial lake... it's so relaxing! If it hadn't been for the vagaries of the weather, we would have been hard put to resist a gallop along the local beaches. You can arrange an excursion from one to several hours (based on a modular setup) that will let you explore the coastal countryside and even kick up the sand along the shore (from 17 September to the end of May, as horses are not allowed on the beach during the summer for obvious reasons).

Another out-of-season option for the more adventurous and experienced is to go on longer outings along the Atlantic Trail (part of which joins up with the Fishermen's Trail), a five-day excursion in which you stay at the farm (as wild camping is still banned in Portugal). For more variation, another five-day adventure takes you both to beaches and to cork oak woodlands, while the farm also offers beginners' workshops for children. There's something for everyone!

The bonus for vanlifers: if you want to go horse riding, you are also allowed to stay overnight on the grounds and take advantage of the facilities including the bathrooms, lounge, bar and Wi-Fi access!

♫ *Wave - The Midnight*

Great addresses we found

Marquês - Cervejaria e Marisqueira

Largo Marquês de Pombal 10,
7520-437 Porto Covo

A really cute little place. The 'Marqueses', a house speciality, are definitely worth a try: an almond-based pastry featuring orange and strands of courgetti (i.e. courgette spaghetti).

Herdade do Pessegueiro

37°49'50.1"N | 8°46'51.2"W

To arrange a tailor-made horse-riding excursion in the northern part of the Sudoeste Alentejano e Costa Vicentina Natural Park.

Around Lisbon

Our tour of southern Portugal has now come to an end. The same can be said of the good weather as we experience our first rainfall since starting this trip while we drive the last few kilometres along the Alentejo coast.

Despite a certain apprehension due to the Algarve's reputation for being full of tourists all year round, we were really taken by this region. Although some parts are indeed crowded even in the off season, it isn't difficult to find relatively wild areas well suited to all kinds of adventures.

The region that awaits us next is very different because we are getting close to Lisbon, the country's capital. We are gripped by a sense of excitement as we have never visited the 'Big Lettuce' before (one of the city's nicknames due to its importance as a lettuce-growing area when the Muslims controlled the Iberian peninsula) and we can't wait to explore its streets and soak up the atmosphere. Lisbon, here we come!

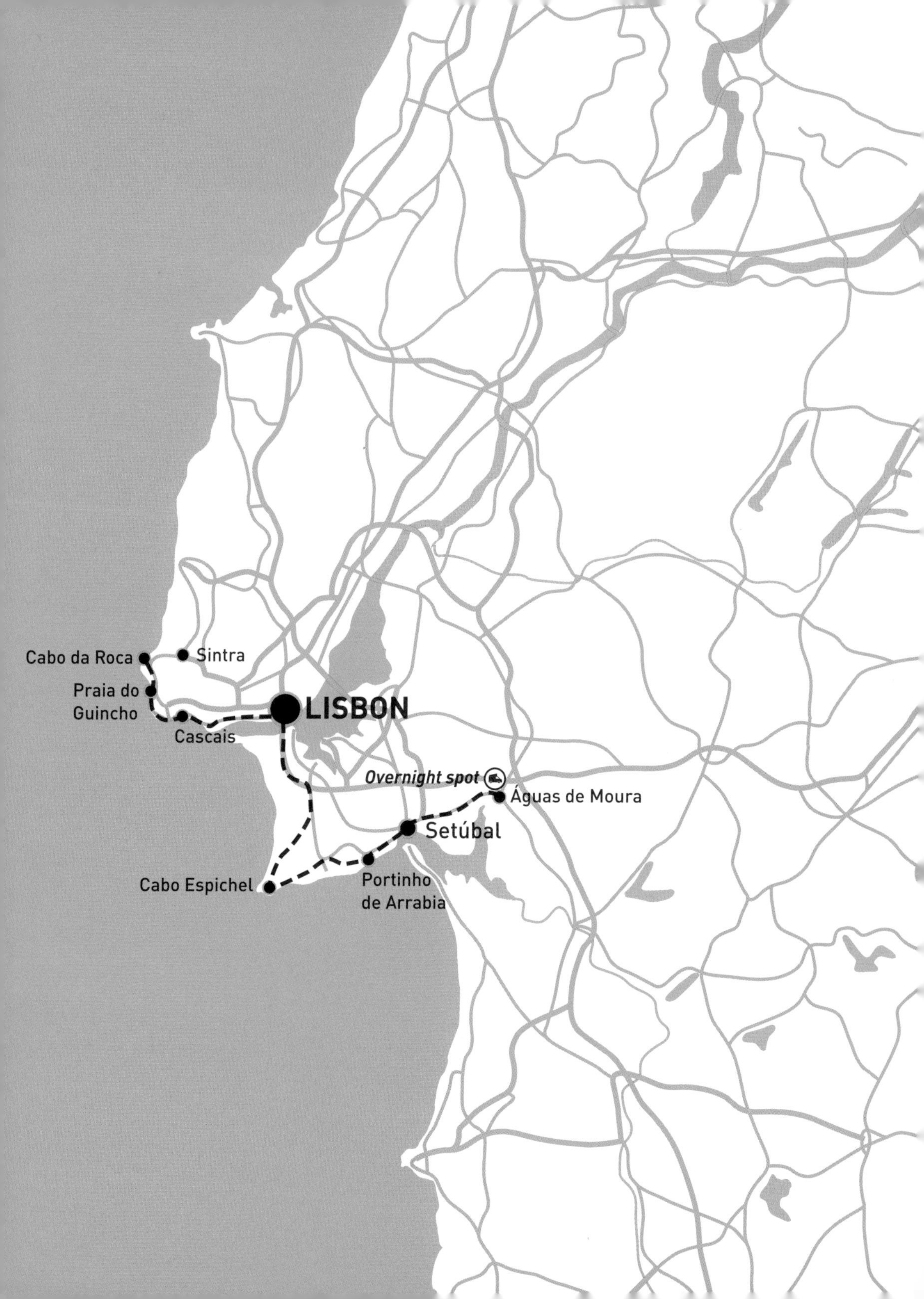
Cabo da Roca
Sintra
Praia do
Guincho
LISBON
Cascais
Overnight spot
Águas de Moura
Setúbal
Cabo Espichel
Portinho
de Arrabia

From Setúbal to Lisbon

For most fans of the converted camper van, being on the road is all about immersing yourself in nature. Even so, you can't really visit Portugal without making a detour via its capital. As our next appointments are all arranged in the vicinity of Lisbon, we enjoy a day's break by driving to the city of a thousand colours via a coastal route through the Arrábida Natural Park. We have the time so let's make use of it!

We wake up at the foot of the impressive Whistler Tree, one of the oldest cork oaks in the world, located east of Setúbal. Then we head south-west along the coast, initially on the N10-4 as far as Praia da Rasca, then on the N379-1. It's a winding route, so it's one to do when you're not in a hurry, all the more so if you want to stop at the various beaches dotted along the way (Comenda, Figueirinha, Creiro). While camper vans are generally forbidden from parking along the road, all these beaches have car parks that allow vans (during the day only).

After managing some challenging bends, we turn off the road and drive to the tiny village of Portinho da Arrábida (38°28'31.7"N | 8°59'03.7"W), built on a dead-end road going in the opposite direction. It's a charming spot that we'd recommend getting to very early if you want to get something to eat or spend the day there: there are only about twenty parking spots, so only the brave will be able to park (for large vehicles, it's best to give it a miss!).

We continue onto Cabo Espichel on the south-west headland of the Setúbal peninsula, not so much for its geographical location as because we want to admire its lovely lighthouse and especially the sanctuary of Igreja de Nossa Sen-

San Francisco - Scott McKenzie

hora do Cabo, built at the start of the eighteenth century. Even though it's partly abandoned, the place is still incredibly impressive and it's well worth a detour.

We take a much more direct route from the cape to the south of Lisbon, while still managing to locate a new ideal spot for a break in the shade of the pine trees. The Herdade do Cabeço da Flauta bordering the N377 is an oasis of shade that will delight travellers wanting to stretch their legs, have a picnic or even walk to Lagoa de Albufeira.
Finally, we end up spending the night at the foot of another giant, parked in front of the Santuário Nacional de Cristo Rei. You can't spend the night within the sanctuary itself, the street in front is relatively quiet even so. During the day, the small park offers sensational views of the River Tagus, the Portuguese capital and the 25 April Bridge, a smaller version of the Golden Gate Bridge. A little bit of Rio, a little bit of San Francisco and an awful lot of Lisbon all in one spot!

Great addresses we found

Herdade do Cabeço da Flauta

38°30'58.0"N | 9°08'43.4"W

The place was empty and quiet when we passed by, perfect for a day lazing about under the pines or exploring the surroundings. All the more so as it is right next to Lagoa Albufeira, a protected wildlife area. On the other hand, if you prefer a lively and electrifying ambience, arrange to visit in July when there is one of the biggest music festivals in the country, the Super Bock Super Rock. This event has attracted fans of rock, indie and alternative music for more than twenty-five years. All-inclusive passes
("including camping at the site"!) can be purchased online several months in advance.

Overnight spot

38°35'11.0"N | 8°41'28.4"W

Sobreiro Monumental de Águas de Moura

At 236 years of age (the average life expectancy of a cork oak is two centuries), the Whistler Tree is one of the oldest and, most importantly, recognized by Guinness as the world's largest sobreiro, or 'cork oak' in English.

A nice thing to visit that owes its name to the many birds that tweet and whistle in its branches during the day, and which has the advantage – especially for camper van travellers – of being surrounded by relatively flat parking spaces!

Travelling by van in big cities

Access bottlenecks, congested city centres, narrow streets, limited, paid parking, the risk of theft... For peace of mind when visiting big cities, we recommend treating yourself to one or two nights at a campsite!

In addition to solving the problem of where to park safely overnight for several nights, this approach will make your trips more efficient! There are in fact often campsites located on the outskirts of major cities, easily accessible and close to a bus or metro stop, so you can get to the centre quickly! Sometimes they even have a bike rental service. Also note that many of them work with the tourist offices, letting you benefit from discounts on your visits or activities.

Last but not least, it will be an opportunity for you to enjoy all the modern comforts: a sink and running water for washing dishes, hot showers, washing machine and dryer, water filling/emptying area, a mains electricity connection and sometimes even Wi-Fi! Moreover, in a country where camping just any old where – 'wild camping' – is forbidden, staying at a campsite will be an opportunity to get out all your equipment (table, chairs, portable stove, washing line, etc.) and to unfurl your awning!

One of our extra tricks: download the Citymapper app which calculates various possible routes on foot, by bike, by public transport (bus, metro, tram, whatever), by taxi and even for chauffeur-driven tours — for many major cities around the world.
Its big advantage is that it provides details and data about each option (distance, duration, calories burned, departure times and so forth). We find it indispensable!

Lisbon by Roammates

Large cities, especially capitals, are rarely suitable for travelling around in a converted van. Lisbon is no exception to the rule, with a city centre that is almost as congested as its access routes. And that's without mentioning the all too regular thefts that take place even during the day, with foreign-registered vans being prime targets because of the high chance of finding some loot. Our advice is to avoid unnecessary stress by pitching at a spot in the Lisboa Camping & Bungalows (22 euros per night for two in low season; double that in mid-summer); from here you can get to the centre of the city founded by Odysseus simply by taking the number 714 bus (30/40 min, 2 euros per trip).

After parking the van amongst the trees in the campsite, we set off to explore Lisbon for the first day. Rather than just going to visit the classic sights that are so prized by tourists, we've decided to draw up a nice list of alternative addresses for you! One small remark en passant: don't feel obliged to stick to our timing or schedule. Coffee, ice cream, pastries, chocolate cake then dinner: there's no real rhyme or reason to the order – it's more a reflection of a vague geographical logic as well as a healthy dose of improvisation. We leave it to you to make something of it!

We get off the bus at its terminus, the Praça da Figueira with its large facades of azulejos, and immediately set off for *Fábrica Coffee Roasters*, Lisbon's first specialty coffee shop of the 'third wave'. Unclear? In short, third-wave coffee shops treat coffee as a high-quality artisanal product (like wine can be in France), putting it on a pedestal of its own. Here, coffee is appreciated in its own right and the preparation leaves nothing to chance. Mind you, it is perfectly adaptable to van life too (see the practical guide on p. 135, Preparing good coffee in a van).

After something hot, it's time for something cold so we stop at *Santini* to shelter from the rain and above all to taste the capital's best ice creams. (Don't miss the Brigadeiro and apple pie flavours!) A few steps then take us to the really cool shop *A Vida Portuguesa*, where all the products (decoration, cosmetics, jams, etc.) are made in Portugal. Staying in the same vein, we take in *Cork & Co.*, where everything is made of cork, also all Portuguese.

A dilemma then arises: whether or not to make the effort to travel all the way out to Belém to taste *pasteis* right where they originated. But the gloomy weather persuades us opt for the simplicity and proximity of *Manteigaria*. And why not follow that up with the best chocolate cake in town, at *Landeau Chocolate* (Rua das Flores 70), a cosy place where there's a perpetual flavour of Christmas and New Year's Eve? The speciality of the house, a genuine ganache paradise, is to die for.

To put the icing on the cake for a day that's all about gluttony, we go to the restaurant *A Provinciana*, recommended by Carlos of Lisbonne Autrement (lisbonneautrement.com), a former Parisian journalist who became a French-speaking Lisbon guide, whom we first met on the bus and then again at *Cork & Co.* You couldn't make it up!

This time, there is no question of refinement or designer influences. The atmosphere is great and it makes an admirable end to our reconnaissance mission in the heart of the capital!

Great addresses we found

A Vida Portuguesa

R. Anchieta 11, 1200-087 Lisboa

A trip in its own right This magnificent address is an all-in-one grocery shop, drugstore, card shop, cannery, decorator's store, tableware and toy shop... It offers articles rooted in tradition that have nurtured the daily lives of the Portuguese "since for ever" (according to the motto on the A Vida Portuguesa logo: *desde sempre*).

Fábrica Coffee Roasters

R. das Portas de Santo Antão 136,
1150-269 Lisboa
R. das Flores 63, 1200-193 Lisboa

Open every day from 08:00 to 18:30

A Provinciana

Tv. do Forno 23, 1150-193 Lisboa

Here, the father is behind the counter, the mother in the kitchen and the daughter is serving in the dining room! All the guests are bundled together in a warm atmosphere; the service is efficient and the prices are unbeatable (between €5 and €6 on average for a dish). The cuisine is simple and delicious and the portions are generous. If the place is never empty and the locals are jostling each other, it's often a good sign.

Making good coffee in a van

There are 'lots of ways to make coffee, but few of them give a satisfactory result and are really suitable for van travel. Fortunately for you, Clémence has a real passion for this particular delicacy and especially for slow coffee, so we're constantly on the lookout for new roasters, new flavours and new techniques to perfect our morning ritual. Our favourite so far is the V60 coffee maker.

In addition to the cafetière itself (consisting of a ceramic, glass or plastic filter holder and a container), you will need a gas kettle with a thermometer, digital scales for the coffee, a stopwatch (if not already integrated into the scales) and special V60 filters.

Preparation

Weigh out 18 g of coffee. (That's for one person. Use 30 g for two.)

Fill your kettle and heat the water to 92°C.

Place the container and filter holder on the scales. Wet the filter to remove any taste and heat the container from underneath at the same time. Then empty the container.

Pour the coffee into the filter, taking care to keep the level horizontal.

Set the scales to zero again and start pouring the water, slowly so that you don't get bubbles on the surface. Stop at 50 g and wait 30 seconds. Then continue in the same way up to 100 g and wait 20 seconds.

Repeat the operation one last time until you reach 250 g (or 400 g for two) and wait 2 minutes on the stopwatch (4 minutes for two).

Lisbon by We Hate Tourism Tours

One of the major pleasures of road trips by van is undoubtedly the possibility of a 'total immersion' journey. When you get out of your vehicle, there's no filter – no hotel lobby or whatever. But when we're talking about visiting the Portuguese capital, there is an even higher level of immersion possible: get into the car of a Lisbon native and listen to him tell you all about his city as we drive through the narrow streets of the historic districts. That's the concept on offer from *We Hate Tourism Tours*,

a small company that's the brainchild of Bruno Gomes, a traveller with an atypical profile. Returning to Lisbon after spells in New York and London, in 2008 this former professional footballer began passing the time by showing tourists around his city by car. Operating since the beginning from the revamped premises of the Lx Factory, he set up WHTT in 2010 and gradually built up a heterogeneous team of guides, chosen less for their qualifications than for their personalities and above all for their love and knowledge of Lisbon.

This particular morning, it's Miguel who lets us get into his van (or an open jeep when the weather permits). Another former footballer and the interpreter for the French soccer team during the World Cup in Rio, he did some of his schooling in France before returning to the city of a thousand colours in 1995. His chirpy nature immediately gets us in the mood, and we set off on a three-hour tour of this beautiful city.

♫ *Take Me Out - Franz Ferdinand*

It should also be noted here that three hours is not too much. In between two sharp bends, a swerve up onto a pavement to go round a double-parked taxi and photo stops here and there, Miguel regales us with his memories and knowledge. As well as the history of Lisbon, he reveals the history of its streets. Of the earthquake of 1 November 1755 in which a third of the population perished, and the reconstruction programme that followed, orchestrated by the Marquis de Pombal, a genius who was the forerunner of modern town planning. Of the creation and popularization of the fado, a melancholy musical genre specific to Portugal, by Maria Severa during the nineteenth century. Or, going further back in time, to the great discoveries and Portuguese maritime engineering, often copied but never equalled. And he didn't forget to give us some good addresses for the best Lisbon products either!

Like the other WHTT guides, Miguel loves his city and makes us love it too. Three hours (King of the Hills, 47 euros per person) of exploring Lisbon's nooks and crannies go past in the blink of an eye in an atmosphere that is as informal as it gets and we're sorry to see it end.

We Hate Tourism Tours

R. Rodrigues de Faria 103, 1300-501 Lisboa
Right in the heart of the Lx Factory.

The cork chain, volume 1

Curious as you are, you're bound to be wondering which country is the leading producer of cork. Don't look any further: the answer is obviously Portugal. Which has a definite head start, as it has 730,000 hectares of cork oak woodlands, representing nearly a third of the total area in the world, at almost 2.3 million hectares.

To learn more about the cork industry, we contacted Rui Alves, director of an estate called Charneca do Infantado, which has the largest cork oak wood in Portugal that is under single ownership. While 92% of the woods are privately owned, the company Companhia das Lezírias (founded in 1836 and nationalized after the revolution of 1974), manages this particular cork woodland on behalf of the state.
Rui guides us through the vast property and describes the steps involved in producing high-quality cork. He explains to us, for example, that cork can begin to be harvested when a cork oak reaches 25 years old, with the removal of the bark (by hand) from the same tree being done every nine years. While the final truck with the season's harvest is being loaded, Rui also explains the criteria that define the quality of Portuguese bottle corks (85% of the estate's production), made from bark with the optimum thickness and porosity.

But cork woodland is more just than a lucrative farm: it is above all an ecosystem in its own right. Its exploitation is thus legally protected and encouraged: a properly maintained cork oak absorbs on average twice as much carbon dioxide as other trees (two to four times more than if it is not being cropped). The system of *montados*, created by humans, is based on a precious equilibrium, which Rui demonstrates to us using some simple elements. On the Charneca do Infantado estate, for example, herds of cows graze under the trees, converting the low vegetation into natural fertilizer and at the same time limiting the risk of fire. The cork industry is not only lucrative but also necessary.

Cork produced in Portugal, which is widely used in the wine industry, is also highly valued in the building sector and even in the manufacture of space shuttles, due to its insulating qualities. A small fraction, however, ends up in cute shops, such as at Cork & Co in Lisbon. There, as well as in other shops in the capital, you'll find lots of items made by talented craftspeople, from bags and caps to jewellery and mobile phone cases. You're sure to find a nice eco-friendly souvenir!

As far as the production of wine-bottle corks is concerned, the key cork producers are located in the south of Portugal whereas the factories are concentrated in the north. But don't worry: a visit has been already planned!

From Lisbon to Sintra... and a bit more

After three days spent in the Lusitanian capital, it's time for us to leave this amazing city which managed to captivate our attention and reveal some of its secrets. Rather than heading directly northwards, we are going to make our way back up by driving along the coast.

Once out of the city, we take the coastal road linking Lisbon to Cascais – the Estrada Marginal (or the N6, as the road signs call it). Cascais is a seaside resort that is very busy at the weekend, so the first few kilometres of our Saturday aren't exactly restful. Nevertheless, the route is thoroughly enjoyable, turning right and then left past the pretty beaches. There's no shortage of parking, but depending on the season and the visitor numbers, it can still be difficult to find a space to park. Sights worth seeing: the Praia de Santo Amaro de Oeiras, the Praia de Carcavelos and its Forte de São Julião da Barra, Estoril and its casino (which is said to have inspired Ian Fleming, the spiritual father of James Bond).

As soon as you get past Cascais, it becomes significantly less busy. We make a stop in Boca do Inferno to stare in awe at this stunning chasm, beaten by the waves of the Atlantic Ocean. A spectacle that's made even more fascinating by the autumnal weather. The N247 then takes us to Cabo da Roca, the westernmost point of continental Europe. *Check.*

Peace and Tranquility to Earth - Roudoudou

An awesome spot, although it's very busy and not much respected by tourists. Staying there has recently been forbidden... We continue north without changing our route, stopping here and there, seeing the views and rainbows and surfing spots through the windows of the van, including the magnificent Praia do Guincho.

The same N247 finally takes us close to Sintra, but we decide to leave that road and take its junior partner, the N247-3. This small and narrower road – sometimes very narrow – winds through the eucalyptus forests of the Sintra-Cascais Natural Park, in an ambience that is made almost mystical by the November fog. Arriving near Sintra, we discover that the gloomy weather hasn't discouraged the crowds of visitors. Given the thick fog, the virtual impossibility of parking and the many impetuous or even downright careless drivers, we give up on the idea of stopping and continue on our way.

So here are a few ideas for those who really do want to visit the places (Parque e Palácio Nacional da Pena, Castelo dos Mouros, Chalet e Jardim da Condessa d'Edla) that seem to be worth it. The first would be to avoid arriving during the weekend if possible. The second is not to go by van (especially if it's any bigger than Fernão) to avoid stressing yourself unnecessarily. The town of Sintra isn't a good place for parking, so we'd recommend organizing your visit from Lisbon, by train or even by using the services of WHTT (57 euros per person for a seven-hour trip around Cascais, Sintra, etc.).

An architectural curiosity at Praia da Água Doce

38°43'44.6"N | 9°28'29.9"W

If you like poking around and trying to find the right angle to take a picture, you sometimes come across absolute gems. This was the case with Estalagem Muchaxo when we were trying to immortalize the Praia do Guincho. Although the hotel appears to be ageing on the inside, its location is genuinely exceptional and its yellow swimming pool, dug into the rock, offers a unique setting and views of the surrounding area.

La Costa da Prata

A plunge into the streets of Lisbon, swerving around obstacles with a colourful guide, an exceptionally tasty coffee, a dinner surrounded by the locals... We expected a lot from our visit to Lisbon and we weren't disappointed! The Portuguese capital is teeming with life and it'll captivate everyone who goes there. Its surrounding area, largely covered by the cork oak woodlands for which the country is famous, offer an obvious and superb contrast.

But after this city interlude, it is time for us to set off again aboard Fernão. 'Aboard' seems the right word, because it is indeed the ocean that will define our next few days, when we arrive on the Costa da Prata, surfing country par excellence.

To make sure we don't miss the perfect wave, we've opted for the so far infallible strategy of contacting a local, in this case a '*shaper*' with a great reputation in Ericeira and its surrounding area. Hold on, we're going to have fun!

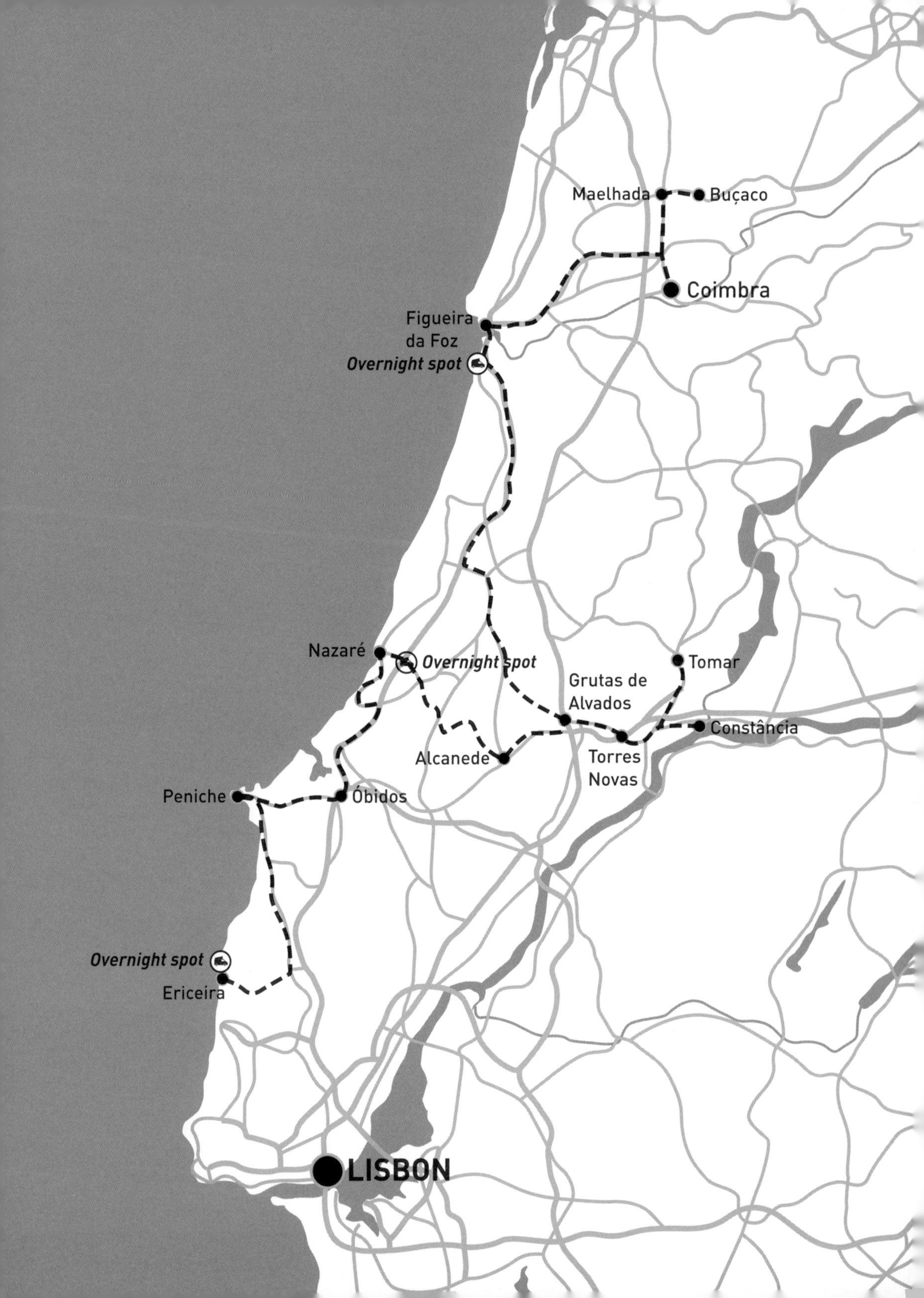
Maelhada
Buçaco
Coimbra
Figueira
da Foz
Overnight spot
Nazaré
Overnight spot
Tomar
Grutas de
Alvados
Constância
Alcanede
Torres
Novas
Peniche
Óbidos
Overnight spot
Ericeira
LISBON

Ericeira's boards

Ericeira is a surfing town. At least that's what most of its inhabitants would claim. And to tell the truth, there was really no need to ask them, as surfing is omnipresent wherever our eyes wander, from shops dedicated to the sport to cafés that include it in their signs or decor.

For connoisseurs: the town can even claim to be the home of Wavegliders. When it's put like that, it probably doesn't mean much to you, but Nico – the founder of the brand – is an icon in the small world of surfboard manufacturing! Between two boards (fully handmade from start to finish, if you please), the *shaper* welcomes us in his workshop to tell us about his journey.
And what a journey! Originally from Lisbon but living in Ericeira for about ten years, Nico has been everywhere, seems to have met everyone, with surfing as a permanent theme. He started out on the waves at the age of fourteen. He made his first board – '*shaped*' it – in the family garden two years later. And he started to learn, find his influences, his mentors, working for a while in Spain and for a few months in France. His touch soon made him an outstanding shaper and he worked for ten years manufacturing high-performance boards.

After a decade in that world, though, Nico could no longer recognize his own touch in his work. He had a manufacturing production line but he was longer creating. So he left his job in 2009 to found Wavegliders, which immediately took off thanks to his reputation. Very quickly, his passion for surfing culture ("surfing's a sport for big kids"), tradition, respect for heritage and his desire to keep the spirit of the pioneers of surfing alive while making his own

Nothing Else Matters - Metallica

contribution, gave him the opportunity to grow and swap ideas with the few real artists in the field who still make their boards by hand. After ten years, Wavegliders' track record is impressive! On the one hand, Nico's reputation now lets him represent various designers internationally. On the other hand, the company boasts production figures of around 5,000 boards in total (15,000 by Nico in his lifetime), selling at between 700 and 2,500 euros apiece, always made to order, to surfers from all over the world.

And also in the town where his heart now is, Ericeira. While his boards had always been more likely to find takers among the passing pilgrims, who generally made the journey especially for him, Nico has been creating boards for the local community for the past two years. That community, previously very closed, has gradually opened up to the outside world under the influence of travellers who have come to mix with local surfers. Nico now supports the town's club and offers boards as a prize at local competitions. Note to passing vanlifers who surf: if you don't have the opportunity to win one of them and want to buy one, it takes three to four weeks to make a board... So think ahead!

But above all, don't hesitate to visit Nico at the shop in the heart of the town, or at the workshop a few kilometres away. Just for the character – impassioned and exciting. On top of that, he knows his region well and will direct you to his favourite spots, such as the beaches of Ribeira d'Ilhas, Foz do Lizandro or São Julião. Or he can also advise you on the best spots in town for drinking a coffee, at *The Mill* or the *Casa das Três* (tried and approved!), or a glass of something at the *Jukebox* or *Hemingway's*, or a toasted sandwich at the *Taberna Lebre*. People who want a bit of summer fun won't be disappointed. For a bit more peace and quiet and even better waves, September, October or even early November are better!

Wavegliders Surf Shop

R. Mendes Leal, 2655-319 Ericeira

A shop dedicated to surfing culture: boards, clothing, accessories, books, etc.

Overnight spot

38°57'41.8"N | 9°25'10.9"W

Ericeira

It's not too difficult to find a parking space in the centre of Ericeira (at least in the off-season!) so that you can explore its charming streets for an afternoon. A little bit of a search, which we have done for you, even lets you stay overnight in almost total peace and quiet!

Go to the small car park next to the restaurant *Esplanada Furnas*, in front of the Parque de Santa Marta, where you can admire the sunset and spend the night with your wheels virtually in the water, enjoying the gentle sound of the waves breaking on the rocks just a few metres away. There's nothing better for getting you into the surfing atmosphere of the town.

Get aboard for Peniche

It's a small world — sometimes surprisingly so. During our trip along the coast, we were keen to organize a waste clean-up session and it just so happens that through two totally distinct networks of connections, we are both acquainted with Mélanie. This particular young woman, Portuguese by birth, is in charge of the Alpes-Maritimes branch of the Surfrider Foundation association, which specializes in coastal cleaning. And we should tell you she's not kidding when it comes to organization!

She didn't just put us in touch with the local branch of Surfrider. No, she came straight out all the way here to meet us. And that's why, when we arrive in Peniche late on a Monday, we meet up with Mélanie – who loves the town – for a first evening with her friends. A great bunch consisting of João, Afonso and Gonçalo (three cousins), Daniel and Pedro.

We find this merry band at the Surfcastle, a small hundred-year-old castle refurbished as a guesthouse and surfing school, family owned and managed by João. A sublime spot where a relaxed atmosphere reigns all year round thanks to the good humour of our hosts and new friends, and which seems to ringing with laughter all the time.

The next day, after a quick breakfast at Mélanie's, we join Lisa (a.k.a. Lizzy Artwork) who is an illustrator by profession and head of the Peniche branch of Surfrider at the Praia Cova de Alfarroba. After divvying up the equipment and the tasks, we walk the dunes for two hours, collecting small bits of plastic, bottles, wipes, corks, packaging and fishing-net remnants. It's painstaking work, as well as gratifying and edifying, and it ends under a torrential downpour – but with everyone still in a good mood. To recuperate, Afonso and Gonçalo take us to the restaurant Toca do Texugo ("The Badger's Den"... work that one out!), where the dishes exclusively use fish caught the same morning. Delicious!

We say goodbye to our new mates after a last afternoon strolling around and a small jazz session at Afonso's A'MAR Estúdio. (Don't be afraid to take your instrument along and jam with this talented double bassist!) But we still spend the night and the next day in Peniche. An opportunity for us to explore and find one last friendly and inspirational place to stay, the Surfers Lodge Hotel in Ferrel. So comfortable and cosy that it's hard to tear yourself away from your sofa!

Great addresses we found

Toca do Texugo

Estr. Marginal Norte, Caminho do Outeiro, 2520-605 Peniche

You choose your fish from the catch of the day before taking a place at your table in the big room amidst a cheerful Portuguese hubbub! Allow between €13 and €18 for a dish.

Surfcastle

Avenida do mar 186, 2520-010 Ferrel

Surf School & Camp. Equipment hire on the spot from €25 a day. As regards the B&B side of things, the three cousins have managed to preserve the spirit of the place. There is a casual atmosphere and the view of the Costa da Prata (Silver Coast) is awesome. From €45 per person per night.

Nosso Mar - SEA Groove

Leaving your spot cleaner than you found it

When on a road trip, the minimum requirement is to leave nothing behind: no harmful traces of our passing, no waste. That's the baseline.
But it's also possible to do more. By putting on gloves, picking up the junk on the ground and helping a little to erase the passing of others too.
And beyond that, as we did in Peniche, you can organize a clean-up, spontaneously amongst yourselves or set up a few weeks beforehand through an association such as the Surfrider Foundation. Their #oceaninitiatives are open to everyone (to participate and/or organize) and they help you create a framework for your activity by providing the teaching tools plus the platforms needed to maximize the impact.

Here are a few other eco-gestures that can easily be incorporated into your van trip:
• Reduce your purchases of plastic, single-use and/or packaged products. Reduce your waste in general. For instance, use tote bags and bulk bags instead of plastic bags. Replace plastic bottles with reusable containers and cling film with reusable beeswax wraps and cotton canvas wraps.
• Separate out your waste and dispose of it in the appropriate bins and containers.
• Use products that are 100% natural and biodegradable. If you're really motivated, you'll even be able to craft your own products.
• Economize on water. If you're travelling with a 40-litre tank, you have to watch your water consumption anyway. Take the opportunity to develop some good habits! Our eco-gesture when preparing meals: fill a small salad bowl with water and wash all our fruit and vegetables in it. Then pour it over our dirty dishes later to rinse them. You can also use seawater or water from a river or stream to do the washing up and then rinse with your clean water.
• Eat local and seasonal produce. There's no lack of local and farm produce in Portugal, at the markets of course, in the *mercearias* and even in the supermarkets.

When the world's become your garden, it's like your own home and you want to keep it clean and healthy. Things you might not have seen before jump out at you and you can no longer ignore them. So you act and, little by little, the effect radiates and people around you start to act too.

If you want to go further, please visit the websites of the Surfrider Foundation. Created in 1990 by a group of surfers who wanted to look after their playground, the organization and its 2,000 volunteers in over 40 branches are working to protect the ocean and coastline in 11 countries: see https://surfrider.eu/

As for us, we also learned a lot by visiting their Ocean Campus site with resources about the ocean and sustainable development. A goldmine of information and ideas.

A jump in time

We leave the coast for a bit and head inland for the Serras de Aire e Candeeiros Natural Park. It covers 38,900 hectares and is best known for what's under the ground: on the one hand some 1,500 caves, and on the other the fact that it is the largest freshwater reservoir in the country. This is, for instance, where some of the water that has supplied Lisbon for two centuries comes from!

From Peniche, we go to the park via the small town of Óbidos, whose fortifications and fortress are reckoned to date back to the Moorish occupation. A great site for a short visit that won't take you more than a couple of hours. There's paid parking at the foot of the ramparts and free parking is available on the far side of the old aqueduct. The first one of these is shaded, so it's the one to pick if you come in the summer. The walkway running round the town wall offers some beautiful views over the roofs of the town, the castle and the surroundings. Worth doing at sunset if possible.

We then soon get to the park. The first stop is in Alcanede, in the heart of a disused quarry, to see the Pegadas de Dinossauros em Vale dos Meios (*pegadas* means 'footprints'). You can wander about the site as you please, following not only in our footsteps but above all in the footsteps that dinosaurs left in the stone many millions of years ago! Just thinking that those impressive creatures have trodden the same ground is mind-boggling and will undoubtedly affect you.

Because the drizzle is now turning into serious rain, we decide to take shelter. What better way is there to do that than to descend several dozen metres underground? Nothing beats that. Our advice: rather than the Grutas de Mira de Aire, which are located in the town of the same name and widely known (and consequently very busy), you could instead go for the Grutas de Alvados, lost in the middle of nowhere and just as impressive (entry is €6 per person, or as a combined ticket with the Grutas de Santo António for €9.40).

Formed by the infiltration of rainwater, a small proportion of the cave system has been known to the region's shepherds since the seventeenth century. But it was only during the second half of the twentieth century that the veil was really lifted on their secrets, revealing several halls decorated with endless stalagmites and stalactites and still, undisturbed small pools. With a maximum depth of 42 m, the visit (which takes about 20 minutes) is ideal both in rainy weather and in the summer heat.

A few kilometres away, a short and easy walk (about 300 m) to the Fórnea de Porto de Mós will give you a breath-taking view of the largest natural amphitheatre in Europe. And to make your visit even more memorable, you can also go to the Centro Hípico De Alcaria if you want to get to the site on horseback (a six to seven-hour ride for experienced riders, €123 per person).

Or you can go back to a more medieval atmosphere when you leave the park, visiting the Convento de Cristo, which is an integral part of Tomar's fortress. A wonderful monument, a legacy from the time when the Knights Templar were trying to reconquer and defend the region against the Moors in the twelfth century. In the same vein, it is also possible to admire the Castelo de Almourol from the road. It was also rebuilt by the Knights Templar, two years after the castle of Tomar.

Finally, for those who want to get some fresh air into their lungs, the Zêzere Park activity centre just is the place. Situated in the small town of Constância where the Tagus and the Zêzere rivers meet (we left the latter near its source in the Serra da Estrela), it offers a good number of nautical and other activities (stand-up paddling, kayaking, climbing etc.), as well as the possibility of camping (€11.10 for two adults in a van in the low season and not very much more expensive in the summer). You can even just take a shower (2 euros per person) and leave!

Great addresses we found

Pegadas de Dinossauros em Vale dos Meios

39°27'28.1"N | 8°49'15.5"W

Go and investigate the thousands of footprints left here in parallel tracks a hundred and sixty-eight million years ago (Middle Jurassic) by herbivorous four-legged dinosaurs (unclear tracks) and carnivorous two-legged dinosaurs (the three-toed tracks in our photos). Mind-blowing!

Overnight spot

39°28'35.0"N | 8°20'28.4"W

Zêzere Park/Camping Constância

Zêzere Park is a great base for anyone who loves to go out on the water or wants to visit the Serras de Aire e Candeeiros Natural Park, the castle at Almourol or the towns of Tomar and Santarém. Although it is open to vans, tents and mobile homes all year round, equipment hire and access to leisure facilities are only available for travellers in the summer months.

An impromptu convoy

Travelling by van gives you not only opportunities to cocoon yourself but also to open your doors and make unexpected, often unforgettable encounters. In December 2018, when we were on a road trip to Galicia, we met Florian when were shared an overnight spot with him at the foot of Ilbarritz castle. One thing led to another and our Basque break turned into ten days spent with this full-time vanlifer (he lives in his van permanently), photographer, surfer in his spare time and coffee lover. We had an immediate click that already hinted at future meet-ups here and there. And why not in Portugal? We received a message a few days ago from 'Flo', who was driving towards the Algarve in search of sunshine. It was too much of a coincidence: a meet-up was a must!

We choose Costa de Lavos as the place to wait for our comrade, next to a huge beach with rollers that definitely look tempting. We pick up some rubbish here and there, get a surprise footbath from a rogue wave, and our mate joins us at the end of the afternoon, just in time to enjoy a splendid sunset that sets the horizon ablaze. The wind is getting up and it encourages us to huddle the vans against the walls of the first houses, but there is no shortage of places in this charming little seaside town. After sharing our victuals and a few drinks, all we have to do is go 'upstairs' to bed and rest before further adventures.

The next day, we leave to explore Figueira da Foz and its surroundings. Situated on the

coast, between a few hills and the Mondego (Portugal's largest river, which has its source in the Serra da Estrela), the town is separated from the ocean by an enormous beach that will delight holidaymakers.
As far as we are concerned, the wind and the rain beating down that day are a great excuse to warm up with the excellent hot, thick chocolate served by the *A Pharmácia* cafe. We'd recommend accompanying it with a scone or a *pastel de nata*!

Then it's time for refreshments, an opportunity for us to give Flo some practical and gastronomic advice about the local services and products that you mustn't miss in the supermarkets. The *pãos* (breads) and *empadas de frango* (chicken pies) at the Lidl, the wide selection of cheeses from the Portuguese *serras*

Bicycle - filous ft. klei

(mountains) at Pingo Doce, the launderettes at Intermarché or the water filling and emptying stations and parking spaces reserved for campers at Continente supermarkets. We have in fact set our sights on two of them that evening, because even if they don't offer an unobstructed view of anything more than the goods delivery entrance, they have the merit of providing us with a welcome refuge, especially after the previous night featured two changes of location in the wee small hours, as the wind was whipping the canvas on the roof about violently... Travelling in a van also means knowing how to adapt!

The next morning, soft rays of sun wake us up and encourage us to get up and enjoy the day to the full. So we set off to discover Buarcos, the next small village along. Fernão and Pistachio (Flo's van) turn a few heads as we expertly weave our way through narrow streets punctuated by pretty, colourful facades.

Then we continue on our way along the coast. After two short stops – one at the Miradouro do Cabo Mondego for the view of Figueira da Foz and another at the eponymous *farol* (lighthouse) – the N109-8 takes us to the Serra da Boa Viagem. Despite being affected by the hurricane of 2018, this wood of pines, cedars and eucalyptus is a small marvel for anyone looking to find a little freshness in the heart of summer. Maintenance work is being done in the low season because so many trees are still falling, so we are not able to cross it. But if you do have the opportunity, though, we invite you to go there on our behalf and experience the natural, verdant arch that has grown above the road. It should be somewhere near the Miradouro da Bandeira.

A Pharmácia

R. Liberdade 96, 3080-168 Figueira da Foz

For a hot drink (the homemade hot chocolate is to die for!) accompanied by a *pastel de nata* or a scone.

Miradouro do Cabo Mondego

40°10'44.8"N | 8°54'15.3"W

For a view of Figueira da Foz and the whole coast!

Costa de Lavos

40°05'25.6" N | 8°52'34.1" W

There are a few places along the beach to enjoy the sunset at the end of the day. Small van sizes only so as not to block the views of the people behind. Awesome view of the ocean. Overnight stays possible. Toilets and showers by the beach in the high season.

An encounter with a local figure

A few days ago, while we were talking with Nico in Ericeira, he gave us the contact info for one of his friends. "If you're going through Figueira da Foz, look up Eurico Gonçalves," he advised us. "He's a real character." And we followed his advice, naturally. If there's one thing we're always interested in, it's real characters!

After exchanging some rather vague messages, we finally manage to meet Eurico at one of his favourite haunts in the town. We arrive a little early and are greeted by the broad smile of the owner of the premises, the bar-restaurant *Gato Preto*, which is very popular with the locals. No sooner have we explained that we are waiting for Eurico than we're immediately offered the grand tour! We are already getting on like a house on fire when the elegant silhouette of our formerly virtual and now very real interlocutor appears at the end of the street. Full beard, pale trousers, black blazer, permanent smile... and a crazy charisma!

Our bonus tip for blending in at a Portuguese bar: order a*copo de três*, a glass of wine in Portuguese format. The *três* refers to the three fingers used to measure the amount of red wine.

We try as best we can to learn a little more about him, his activities and his past. The guy's a surfer, obviously, but remains enigmatic about what he does. "I hang out at the beaches," "I connect with the people around me," – we get vague answers like that. Nevertheless, we do end up learning that he chairs an association called ADMS (Associação de Desenvolvimento Mais Surf – the 'Development and Surf Association'), which aims to promote the practice of surfing and other water sports while developing and enhancing the local natural assets. But no more questions for now, we're boarding Fernão again. Eurico is taking us to his favourite surfing spot!

It's late in the afternoon when we arrive at this 'all-in-one' spot, the Praia do Cabedelo. Ideal for catching some great waves of between 1 and 4 m, spending the night (as it is not only allowed there but also very easy to park), having a drink at the *Surf Bar*... Or you can come and shape a surfboard, if you have the will or the skill. No problem if not: you can learn how on the association's premises! Above all, crucially, if you're in the area around the end of August, you can take part in the Gliding Barnacles festival organized by ADMS throughout the beach area.

Eurico leaves us for an hour to go surfing with one of the association's shapers, during which time we meet two Austrian travellers. When he comes back out of the water, our group has grown a bit in the meantime, as we chat about what's so great about surfing, the festival, everyone's individual projects and more. As it's getting late and we're starting to feel hungry, Eurico invites us to join him and his friends to test out a pizzeria, *Il Camino*. Passed with flying colours! The pizzas are delicious, and we also end up learning a bit more about our guide, who turns out to be a former Portuguese longboard champion (2008), no less! A character who is definitely full of surprises.

The Gliding Barnacles festival

First seeing the light of day in 2014 under the aegis of Eurico and some friends at Figueira da Foz, this surfing festival is totally different, a kind of indefinable UFO where Italian cooks rub shoulders with French musicians, Brazilian and Korean surfers and Australian photographers, a festival that blends surfing, creative arts, music, and above all a general good mood — we already want to come back next year.

"What makes our festival unique is the people," says Eurico humbly as he tells us the story of his project. Here, although there is a competition, it gets relegated to the background. Moreover, whether you are a seasoned surfer or just a beginner, you will get to ride a wave. You can enjoy gigs during the four to seven days of the festival or take in a piano

recital on the beach, feast on international cuisine (or even get behind the stove, who knows!), learn to shape a surfboard or take an impromptu surfing lesson, taste one of the creations of the *Surf Brewing* microbrewery (whose IPA won an award among 1,100 beers in a competition in Germany and whose profits go entirely to ocean conservation)... and – a really interesting plus for us – you can park your van for the duration of the festival!
What does taking part cost? That's up to the visitors, who pay what they want for unlimited access to the whole area. The only requirement is that you smile!

Great addresses we found

Gato Preto

R. Alfândega 14, 3080-074 Figueira da Foz

Eurico's headquarters, where you can share tapas and a *copo de três* with friends! A wonderful and very distinctive place.

Overnight spot

40°08'25.1"N | 8°51'45.7"W

Praia do Cabedelo

Praia do Cabedelo may not be the most bucolic spot, but it is recommended by Eurico Gonçalves, former longboard champion of Portugal. What more do you need?

Situated not far from what was undoubtedly once an industrial port, the location is absolutely ideal. That is on the one hand thanks to the peace and quiet, as the area is now almost deserted except for a campsite and two café-restaurants. And on the other hand, it's thanks to the beach in question, a place favoured by local surfers including our champion.

All you have to do is park in the unpaved car park, literally a few metres from the ocean, and enjoy the view and the waves. For more entertainment, don't hesitate to come back at the end of August, when the Gliding Barnacles festival takes place here.

Coimbra by water

This 'small' family business has been organizing canoe and kayak trips on the Mondego for more than thirty years. The Penacova-Torres descent (the one we did – 18 km) will set you back about €22.50 per person. For the longer one (only in high season – intermediate level, 25 km), it's €24.50 euros per person and you can also discover Coimbra by water on arrival. It is possible to organize your trip starting and finishing at the Parque do Choupalinho camper van site. Handy!

O Pioneiro do Mondego

40°11'28.9"N | 8°23'16.8"W

Smile - David Gilmour

Queijadas

Ingredients for 6 queijadas

Oven and grill

6 small moulds

120 g sugar (muscovado in our case!)

30 g butter

2 eggs

70 g flour

250 ml semi-skimmed milk

Coarsely chopped almonds

Preparation

Mix the sugar, melted butter and eggs, then whisk. Add flour and whisk.

Remember that your kitchen will have a great view today and enjoy it for a moment!

Add the milk and whisk.

Preheat the oven to high.

Divide the mixture among the 6 moulds and put them in the oven.

Leave to cook for 30/40 min. Check from time to time until you get the golden colour you want.

Leave to cool and enjoy!

La Mata Nacional do Buçaco

Perched up high, almost lost on the outskirts of the small town of Luso (about ten minutes away on foot), the Mata do Buçaco, also spelled Bussaco, is one of Portugal's little-known treasures. A sublime woodland 1.5 x 1.0 kilometres (105 hectares) nestled in the Serra of the same name and containing more than 250 exotic plant species (700 in all), it is one of those places where you feel that you're disturbing the tranquillity when you enter, where entrancing nature is blended with a wealth of history and heritage.

Occupied by Benedictine monks since the sixth century, the bishopric of Coimbra took possession of it during the eleventh century before entrusting it to the Discalced Carmelites six hundred years later. It was the monks who turned it into the superb place that you can visit today, surrounding the wood with a wall, building a monastery (since transformed into a palace), a convent, chapels and hermitages that can be discovered along the paths that cut furrows through the woods. It's full of treasures to discover on foot, by bike or in a van, and it is well worth spending a day or two there.

An added bonus is that the location is perfectly suited to a visit in a van. Entrance is 7 euros (12 euros for a camper van, free for pedestrians and cyclists) and even entitles you to overnight parking in one of the various car parks (P3, at the foot of the Palácio Real, seems to be the most suitable). Of course, after stopping in the rain at the Fonte Fria, we're not about to miss the opportunity to enjoy the woodland in the morning light.

So we set off at daybreak on a walk along the old paths, discovering something every step of the way: a century-old tree, an abandoned

chapel, a reproduction of the Stations of the Cross, or the two papal bulls concerning the Mata, which adorn the gate of Coimbra. The path that loops round the woods, Adernal do Buçaco, offers a good selection of the riches the Mata has on offer and it can be walked in less than an hour.

A small bonus for you: the Cruz Alta, built at the highest point of the Mata, has a car park that can be accessed by van without having to enter the grounds... So you can park there for free and continue by foot in the woods - you can even spend the night there in complete calm!
The general map and details of the various themed paths of the Mata can be found on the website: www.fmb.pt/.

Great addresses we found

Rei dos Leitões

Avenida da Restauração 17, 3050-382 Mealhada

For the local speciality, suckling pig on a spit... There's something à la carte for vegetarians too, but no guarantee that the trip will be quite your thing! Reckon on about €25 per person for an aperitif and the house speciality.

Fonte de São João à Luso

40°22'59.7"N | 8°22'35.2" W

Luso, founded in 1852, has springs that let weary travellers recharge their batteries at the usual spa town facilities (spa, baths) or indulge in the decadent luxury of the adjoining 4-star hotel, the Fonte de São João, just a few dozen metres from the thermal baths. Though neither particularly pretty nor charming, the fountain is the scene of non-stop toing and froing as the locals come to stock up on drinking water in large five-litre bottles. Not so surprising when you consider that Luso mineral water ("as natural as your thirst") is the oldest mineral spring in the country and that bottled water from Luso has been part of Portuguese daily life for 125 years. Our tip: take your bottles and jerrycans!

Porto the Grand

Surfing and the lifestyle that goes with it are omnipresent all along the Portuguese coastline, from one end of the Spanish border to the other. That's even truer of the Costa da Prata, which we have now left.

And even if we didn't have the opportunity to get into the water ourselves, these last few days have nevertheless been marked by surfing, and especially by the people we met in Ericeira and Figueira da Foz – outstanding characters whose generosity will remain with us for a long time to come.

The region of Porto now stretches out before us and a completely different atmosphere awaits. Especially when visiting the Invincible City, its cellars and its lively streets. But before that, let's take you to Aveiro to discover Portugal's little Venice!

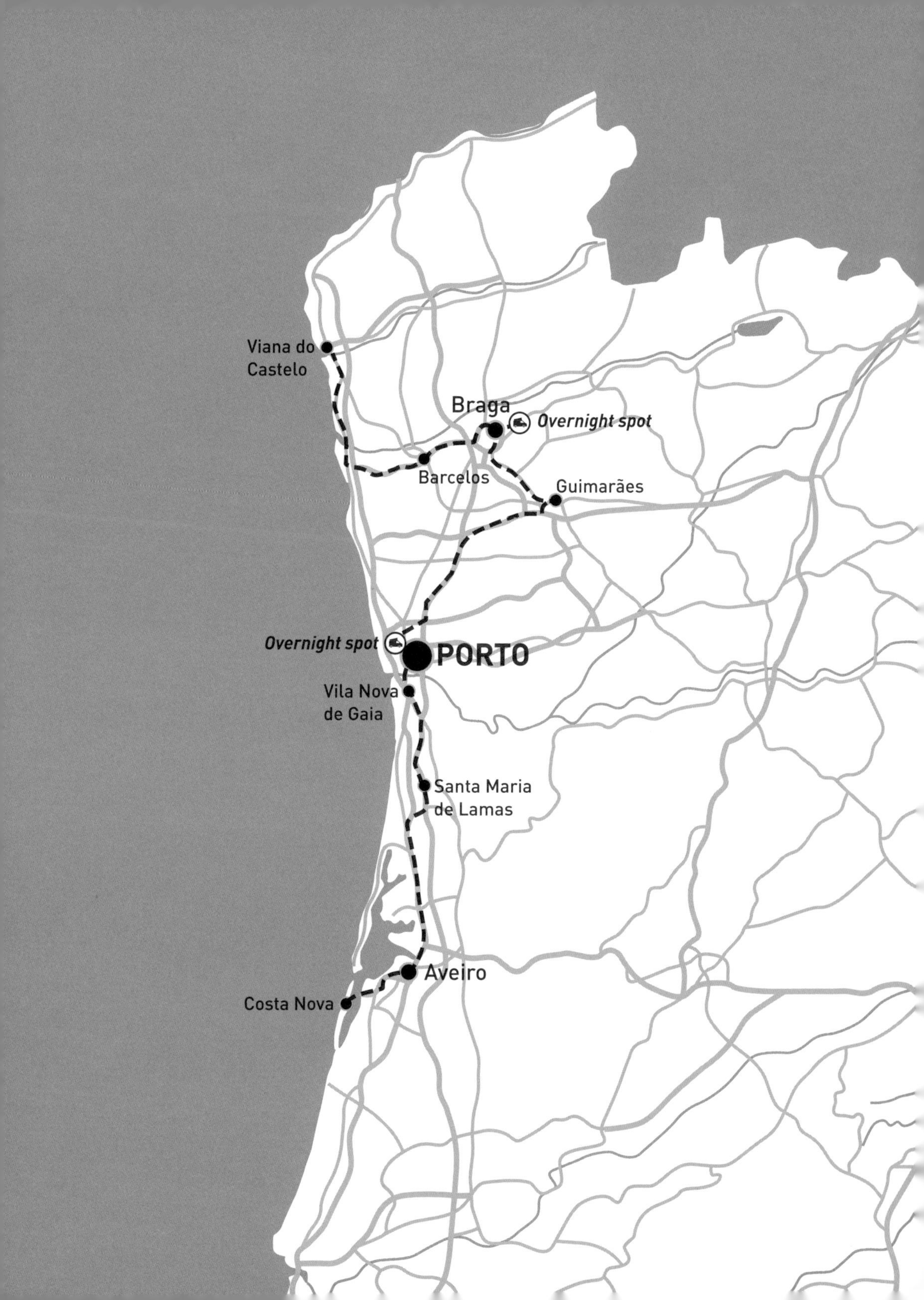
Viana do Castelo
Braga
Overnight spot
Barcelos
Guimarães
Overnight spot
PORTO
Vila Nova de Gaia
Santa Maria de Lamas
Aveiro
Costa Nova

A small town before the big ones

Before diving into Porto, the last major urban area of this Portuguese journey, we decide to get used to the city atmosphere again by making a diversion via Aveiro, which some people call the 'Portuguese Venice'. The first advantage it has over its Italian counterpart is that you can park just a stone's throw from the town centre of Aveiro! So let's see if the rest of the town stands up to the comparison.

And let's be honest, Italy's La Serenissima sets the bar very high. But Aveiro is nevertheless definitely worth a walk around, whether you stroll along its canals (which are certainly less numerous than in the real Venice) or through the maze of small streets with their clusters of colourful little houses that are distinctly reminiscent of Burano, the island in the Venetian Lagoon.

During your walk, go and taste the specialities of the house at *Peixinho*, a confectionery that is famous for its *ovos moles* (and variants), small pastries based on sweetened egg yolks. You can enjoy them on the spot (only at weekends in the low season) or do as we do and take an assortment of them with you back on board the van. If you need to warm up, or simply to balance your diet after the *leitão*, a break at the vegetarian tearoom and restaurant *Raiz* ought to do the trick. We didn't try everything, but everything we did taste was good and prepared with local, organic products!

Once we've done the tour of the town centre, we pick up Fernão again to proceed a little further towards the *farol* (lighthouse), which in addition to being very attractive – with its wide white and pink (faded red?) horizontal stripes – reaches a height of 66 m, making it the tallest lighthouse in the country and the second tallest on the Iberian Peninsula.

Finally, we conclude this short excursion in Praia da Costa Nova do Prado, where picturesque striped houses line the beaches. Originally, in the nineteenth century, these *palheiros* were huge sheds that fishermen stored their gear in. Over time, they have been gradually converted and upgraded into family holiday homes. Originally built using red-painted horizontal planks, these *palheiros* and their descendants are now covered with *azulejos* arranged in wide, mostly vertical bands alternating between white and a bright colour (red, yellow, green or blue). They give the small seaside resort an absolutely magnificent colourful look in the late afternoon light.

Great addresses we found

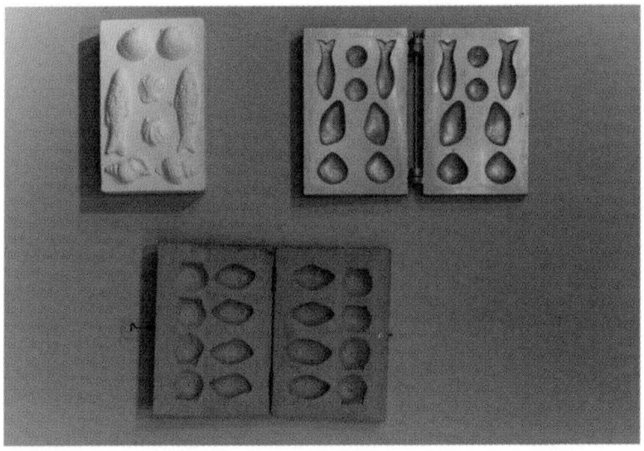

Confeitaria Peixinho

R. de Coimbra 9, 3810-086 Aveiro

For sampling the local pastry specialities based on egg yolks and in particular the famous *ovos moles* in their boxes in the shape of a barrel, shellfish, fish etc.

Cooking in a van

In Fernão, as in most converted vans, the equipment at our disposal is a fridge, cupboards, a table/worktop, a two-ring gas hob, and a small sink with a tap connected to a 40-litre water tank. Pretty much all the equipment you need for cooking!

On the other hand, as in most converted vans, you won't have too much space for storing everything! So here are a few tips for optimizing your space!

Organizing the cupboards

First of all, make sure you've got small tubs for wedging things in place when you're on the move, and organize your drawers and/or cupboards properly. You can even go as far as writing what they contain on their visible side to let you find everything more easily.

The essentials to have in your cupboards:

• A small larder on board with your cooking essentials: salt, pepper, spices, sugar, coffee, tea, pasta, rice, a few jars, stock cubes, etc.
NB: don't forget that Portugal offers a treasure trove of local products: olive oil, dried fruit, flours of all kinds, you name it. So don't take too much stuff!

• A few pieces of crockery and things to eat from, table linen and kitchen utensils. Plates, cutlery, various knives, a cutting board, mugs, bowls, salad bowl, corkscrew, tea ball, scissors, peeler, whisk, wooden spoon, frying pan, saucepan, colander, gas kettle, coffee maker, sponges, tea-towels.

• A gas oven/stove. A table-top cooker for baking cakes, bread, flans, pizzas or any other dish that needs to be toasted or roasted! Since we got ours, our travels have literally had more flavour!

• A small mobile gas stove for cooking outside when you are at a campsite or at an overnight spot that allows it.

Space-saving tricks:

• To unclutter the cupboards and limit the number of times we're getting things in and out, we put the items we use most often in a big basket behind the driver's seat.

• As Martine Camillieri rightly puts it in her book *Never without my Kmion*, promote 'nomadism of uses' wherever you can! In other words, one object = several uses! An eco-cup can be both a glass AND a measuring cup, a plate is a bowl AND a lid, the same cloth can be a tea-towel AND bread wrapping... You get the idea!

Cuisine, cooking and preparation

Once you're perfectly set up, you have everything you need to cook like at home! Except that you aren't at home and the van isn't connected to the gas network. So between the cakes or roasts, here are a few tips to save on your gas consumption!

• Choose minimalist cuisine and/or things that you can eat raw. You're in Portugal, so prepare toasties, bruschettas, wraps and other snacks with local products! It's simple, efficient and delicious!

• If you really want hot meals, go for short cooking times and *al dente* textures. To help you do that, cut your food into strips or small pieces to reduce cooking time. Don't forget to cover your pan when boiling water. Remember that food in a frying pan continues to cook even after the heat has been turned off! Another solution is to go for dishes that are pre-prepared, for example in jars (made at home or bought), which you will only have to reheat and possibly add some rice, pasta or seeds to add some bulk!

Right next to Porto

Let's play our favourite game! If someone says Porto the city, you may quite probably first think of port the fortified wine. And you will certainly learn, as we have, that none of the stages of port production take place in Porto, strictly speaking! It all starts in the vineyards of the Douro region and then in the town of Vila Nova de Gaia, which is opposite Porto on the other side of the river and where we begin our visit.

It would indeed have been difficult to pass through Portugal's second city without visiting the cellars for which it is renowned. Before the trip, we had contacted two of them, Graham's and Cockburn's (belonging to the Symington family), who both responded by inviting us to a tour of their facilities and a tasting. The morning seems likely to be particularly perilous... Our advice (please, we insist): organize your visit to the cellars in the morning, park the van and don't touch it again until the end of the day. A nice smile will probably even let you, as we did, leave the van in a wine shop's car park for the rest of your visit to the city.

The first thing to note, for both Graham's and Cockburn's, is that the names of these labels don't exactly sound Portuguese. The major producers of port, of which Symington is the largest with 26 estates throughout the Douro region, are indeed (mainly) Scottish families, who go right back to the origins of these particular fortified wines. Here's how! We're in the sixteenth century and the British, who are reluctant to do business with France, currently prefer Portuguese wine. The wines don't travel well, though, so they decide to add brandy to prevent the wine from turning bad. Over the years, the British refine the process by adding brandy earlier and earlier during the wine production: the high level of alcohol kills the bacteria, fermentation ceases and it becomes possible to obtain wines that are sweeter but with a high concentration of alcohol. Port wine is therefore a British invention.

On top of the historical anecdotes that João and Tiago (our guides) regale us with, we learn a thousand things during these visits, while enjoying the sumptuous surroundings of the Graham and Cockburn cellars, the latter being particularly massive with almost 1 km of spans between the *pipas* (barrels) and the *balseiros* (vats containing tens of thousands of litres). Our guides describe the successive stages of production, from harvesting grapes on the banks of the Douro and the blending (estates, grape varietals and years) that is done on site, to the transport to Vila Nova de Gaia, putting the wine into casks or barrels for ageing, and finally the bottling.
We discover the various types of port: ruby (red, fresh and fruity) and tawny (spicier and amber-coloured) that are blends of wines from different years, as well as vintage port from exceptional years.

Graham's Port Lodge

Rua do Agro 141, 4400-281
Vila Nova de Gaia

Visit + tasting: between €18.50 and €24 per person for tasting in the attractive main hall. And between €40 and €120 per person for a comfortable session in the Vintage Room. The prices vary depending on the ports selected for each of the tastings (ruby, tawny, vintage). There is the option of a visit without a tasting (for the designated driver, for example) for €13. Reservations: www.grahams-port.com/

The latter are excellent ports for laying down (the others don't improve after bottling) and sometimes only reach their peak after fifty years of ageing! Some of the bottles stored in the cellars are genuine historical objects, including ones dating back to the beginning of the nineteenth century.

At the end of each visit, we are entitled to a tasting, both in amazing rooms. This includes the vintage lounge at Graham's (from €35 per person up to €350 depending on the ports you want to taste). The ports, paired with chocolates made by a port house, are explosions of incomparable flavours. You can find most of the bottles you tasted for sale in the shops at the end of the visit. For the 1815 vintages, on the other hand, you'll probably have to speak directly to the management or go through an auction and brace yourself for a sum including several zeroes.

Cockburn's Port Lodge

R. de Serpa Pinto 346, 4400-307
Vila Nova de Gaia

Visits + tasting: €15 or €23 per person for tasting in the small main hall. And between €35 and €50 per person for a cosy session in the John Smith Room. The prices vary depending on the ports selected for each of the tastings (ruby, tawny, vintage) and on what they are served with (chocolates, pastries or cheeses). There is the option of a visit without a tasting (once again for the designated driver!) for €12. Reservations: www.cockburns.com

On the heights of Porto

Intoxicated by the wealth of information ingested in the Graham's and Cockburn's cellars, we leave the van there and go exploring the capital of the North on foot. From Vila Nova de Gaia, getting to Porto on foot takes fifteen to twenty minutes and you get beautiful views of the Douro, the historic Ribeira district and the Ponte Luiz, built between 1881 and 1886 by Théophile Seyrig (a former associate of Gustave Eiffel of Parisian tower fame).

When we reach the north bank, we are immediately struck by the charm of Porto, its human scale, its houses that seem to be stacked one atop the other and its general atmosphere when the sun makes an appearance. Instead of staying in the tourist zones, we head directly to the Lapa and Boavista districts, located further back from the Douro and therefore requiring a climb of a few dozen metres in altitude, which are quickly dealt with.

The first stop is an attractive shop called Mercado 48 selling a motley assortment of fashion paraphernalia, decorations, souvenirs and works by Portuguese designers, all made entirely in Portugal. Dozens of cafés near the shop catch our eye, each seeming cosier than the next, but we are on a mission and nothing will distract us from it...

Because if Lisbon has its*pastéis de Belém* or *pastéis de nata*, Porto has its own *francesinha* and we absolutely must try it. Just out of curiosity, and because we've still got an empty stomach after our two port tasting sessions. What is a *francesinha*? Although a minority attribute its origin to the Napoleonic invasions, there is pretty much a consensus that the inventor was a certain Daniel David Silva in the 1950s.

Having worked in France, he is thought to have been inspired by the famous croque-monsieur to create a variation and add a sauce to France's famous toasted sandwich. In the Portuguese version, you will find *linguiça* (pork sausage with garlic and paprika), another sausage, ham and fillet of beef or veal between the slices of bread... and it's all covered with melted cheese and bathed in a sauce based on tomatoes, beer and red peppers.

What you have to remember, despite seeming like a random and somewhat excessive stack of ingredients, is that the dish is really very good... and very filling. To get a high-quality *francesinha*, we follow the advice of the locals, which we're transcribing for you here: go for the *Café Luso* (between 8 and 12 euros, depending on the version you choose, and treat yourself to the whole caboodle with egg and French fries while you're at it) and you won't be disappointed! A short trip to *Cremosi* for home-made ice cream or something else sweet concludes a well-rounded day before we set off on new adventures.

Great addresses we found

Mercado 48

R. da Conceição 48, 4050-213 Porto

Small shop offering a wide selection of items by Portuguese designers. Will suit any budget and any taste. Ideal for finding small presents and/or souvenirs.

Café Luso

Tv. da Queimada 10, 1200-365 Porto

To try the *francesinha*, a croque-monsieur in a Portuguese sauce. Go the whole hog and order the version with batata e ovo for €11. There's a lot of it, and it's pretty salty – but delicious!

Overnight spot

41°10'13.5"N | 8°40'47.1"W

Parque da Cidade à Porto

It's always tricky to find a quiet location on the outskirts of a major city like Porto. But nothing is impossible for the brave at heart! And, after several unsuccessful attempts along an often too busy shoreline, we have a solution for you.

The Parque da Cidade, located to the north of the city, solves this problem brilliantly. Although it's right in the heart of a busy area, with a Pingo Doce supermarket for if you need any provisions, the park is very quiet at night. Overnight stays are allowed for recreational vehicles and there are even public toilets available. However, be sure to pick a spot at the bottom left of the car park for maximum peace and quiet, away from the traffic and buses.

The cork chain, volume 2

Just three weeks ago, we were watching the last truck of the 2019 cork harvest leave the Charneca do Infantado estate on its way to Porto. Now that we also have arrived in the Invincible City, it's time to pick up the tracks of the precious bark in order to learn a little more about one of Portugal's flagship industries, the production of cork stoppers.

To do so, we contacted Claudia from Apcor (the Associação Portuguesa de Cortiça), the organization responsible for promoting cork both in Portugal and internationally, who organized a visit to the Sá & Irmão factory for us (€5 per person). We are greeted by Manuel Sá, nephew of the company's founders (it dates from 1976) and himself co-owner of this 'second-line' brand, the first being the undisputed market leader Amorim. The second line consists of major companies capable of managing their production from end to end, the third line consisting of more modest setups that can only handle certain parts of the supply chain, delegating the rest to larger players.

Manuel takes us on a tour of their state-of-the-art factory, leading us through its labyrinthine areas to explain the various stages of the transformation of cork. There is an initial sorting after arrival, as not all the cork can be

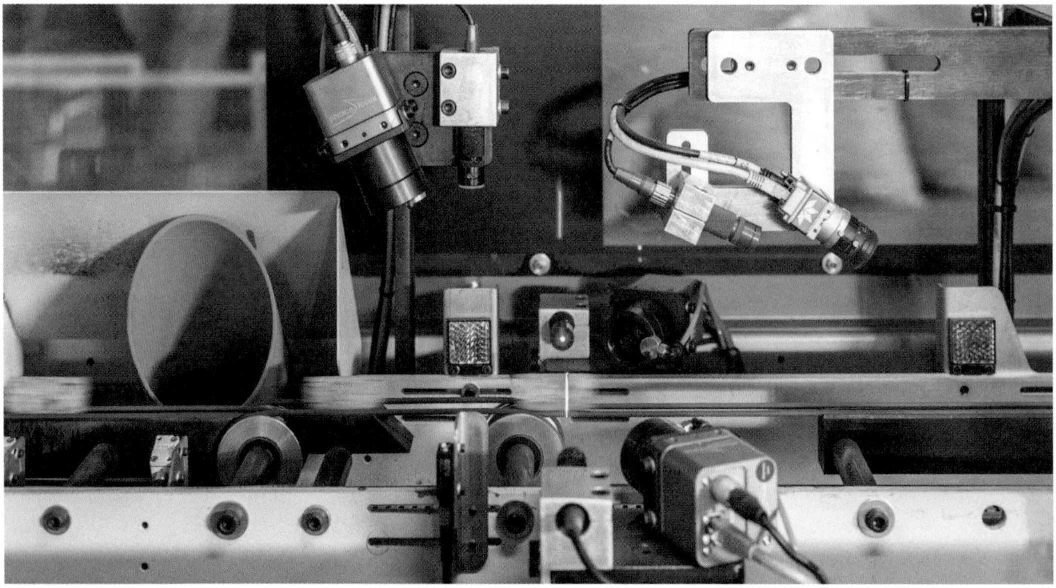

used to make high-quality bottle stoppers (bark from too close to the ground may be contaminated by bacteria, for example), followed by an initial cleaning to get rid of impurities. The cork is then stored in enormous cold rooms and then sorted again, depending on how it is going to be used. And from there on, the story gets a bit technical!

The highest-quality bark can be used to make what are referred to as 'natural' stoppers, i.e. one cut directly from the cork slices, then cleaned again, scanned by a machine that determines the quality before distribution (we told you it got technical!), cleaned yet again and checked (both by smelling and in a laboratory) again and again until they are almost infallibly clean! The lower-quality bark, as well as the off-cuts, will be reduced to granules destined to become 'technical' stoppers, compressed and shaped to seal your champagne bottles.

The choreography of the various production lines is impressive, rehearsed to perfection, controlled from start to finish in order to achieve optimum quality and above all to reduce waste to absolute zero. Even the cork dust is used as fuel! All this allows Sá & Irmão to produce almost a million cork stoppers a day, with prices ranging from 20 eurocents to 1 euro.

After saying goodbye to Manuel, who has to go to Bordeaux (what a coincidence!), we follow Claudia to the magnificent APCOR premises, an almost inexhaustible source of information about this fantastic material and its multifarious applications. It is also an exhibition site where it is possible to admire (and even buy in some cases) the creations of various designers almost entirely made of cork: tableware, fashion, accessories, toys, you name it... Every item looks like a work of art and you're sure to find a souvenir to your taste.

APCOR: Cork Welcome Center

Avenida Comendador Henrique Amorim
580 P, 4536 – 904 Santa Maria de Lamas

Cork Experience Tour: guided tour on the theme of cork in a cork factory or at a producer's. Reckon on €5 per person (for groups from 5 to max. 40 people). Open all year round except during August. By reservation only; for more details go to www.apcor.pt/en/ or send an e-mail: info@apcor.pt

Staying connected as you travel

In a world where most of our electrical equipment is recharged via USB ports, travelling by van is very convenient!
In Fernão, as in most recreational vehicles, driving recharges the accessory battery, letting you take advantage at every stage of your journey of a 12V supply (transformed up to 220V by a dedicated converter in some models), with total autonomy.
Add to this the possibility of sharing the 4G of your telephone package (at no extra cost for Europeans, but Brits may need to check!) and there you are, right in the heart of nature but with all your essentials at your fingertips, plugged in and connected! And if you want to go off-grid for a while, switch to 'airplane mode': there's no need to have everything enabled just because you can!

For those whose activities require an energy-guzzling connection and/or a 220V socket, there are two options:
• Save up your work sessions for a visit to a campsite or a service area that has electricity sockets.
• Go to one of the many *cafetarias* and *pastelarias* that offer free Wi-Fi access and use of their sockets as long as you are consuming something! "Um bica e um pastel de nata por favor!"

Finally, if your 4G package is the limiting factor, it's worth knowing that most buildings and centres open to the public provide their own networks, which are reasonably reliable and efficient.

A sacred transition

Porto is now in our rear-view mirrors, as we begin the last part of our journey, which will take us to the north of Portugal where we will follow the Spanish border from west to east. The Lord guides our route (unless the voice we can hear is our GPS) towards the first stop of the day, the Santuário de Nossa Senhora do Carmo da Penha.

It is located on Monte da Penha, very close to the city of Guimarães, and provides an excellent base where you can park your van (free parking) and go down to visit the city via the cable car that connects the two points (€3.50 per adult, €5 for a round trip, opening days and times vary according to the season). Guimarães is also well worth a visit for the historical heritage that is present in every corner of the town centre: as the inscription on the old city wall claims, *Aqui Nasceu Portugal* ('Portugal was born here'), freeing itself from the Galician yoke in the twelfth century.
In addition to being an ideal stop for a stroll around town, the site of the sanctuary itself is superb, littered with numerous massive granite blocks, some of which have been adapted for climbing. As the car park is huge and flat, it is perfectly possible to spend the night there, while travellers in search of facilities can alternatively find refuge at the campsite.

Head northwest to get to Braga and above all the Santuário do Bom Jesus do Monte. The first sanctuary of the day may have delighted us with its natural charm, but this one's architectural splendour is on a par with some of the world's finest cathedrals. Sufficiently so that it has been classified as a World Heritage Site by UNESCO since July 2019. The basilica and the imposing staircase would impress anyone, and for those who are reluctant to make a major effort, there's an old funicular to save your breath that takes you to the top of the site (€1.20 for a one-way trip, €2 for a return) from the first free car park (it's paid parking at the top, €10 per day in the high season). The lower car park is moreover flat, shady and it looks very much like a perfectly good spot for a nap!

Let's leave the more spiritual theme of today for a moment and treat ourselves to a slice of culture (and cake). Although religion is never far away, as you will see... We make a stopover in Barcelos, famous for its cockerel, one of Portugal's emblems. As legend has it, a pilgrim who was falsely accused of various crimes took a roast cockerel as a witness (admittedly a dubious choice) when he went before the judge, claiming that the aforementioned bird would start singing to prove his innocence. When the cockerel performed just before the hanging, the pilgrim was freed. Legend doesn't tell us what song the rooster chose, but the bird has been a symbol of faith and justice ever since. In addition to this tall story, you will also find superb remnants of the town's rich history, as well as the pastry shop *Casa das Natas* and its excellent *Bolo Rei de frutos secos* (or the *Bolo Rainha*, a delicious Christmas brioche with dried fruit).

Finally, our third and last religious stop of the day is high up in the town of Viana do Castelo, answering to the gentle name of Santuário do Sagrado Coração de Jesus. As its 'sacred heart' name suggests (given that you, like us, now understand Portuguese perfectly), the style is largely inspired by the Sacré-Cœur de Paris. As well as the magnificent basilica of Santa Luzia, you can enjoy a splendid panoramic view of Viana do Castelo, the Eiffel Bridge dating from 1878 and the Atlantic

Ocean. Not to be missed in the fading light of late afternoon! Nevertheless, expect to have to wend your way through a mass of cars and tour coaches.
Having said that, you don't have to get up high to enjoy the area! Numerous superb walks are being upgraded and developed along the Portuguese coast. The Ecovia do Litoral is 73 km in length (some parts still under construction)

that you can walk or cycle, along the Atlantic coast of the Costa Verde. Note that the ten kilometres or so between Viana do Castelo and Afife beach are apparently a really nice stretch that was highly recommended to us.

Heading inland, there's also the Ecovia do Rio Lima trail, running through the heart of a Natura 2000 area (a network of natural or semi-natural sites within the European Union with significant heritage value due to their exceptional fauna and/or flora) and following the river for 70 km as far as Ponte da Barca.

Wooden or concrete footbridges, landscaped dunes, both cultural and heritage-related points of interest, vinho verde tasting, fauna and flora to watch and find, an old railway line, beaches, architectural curiosities... the range of things to discover is vast. Some sections are even themed. Don't hesitate to visit the Viana do Castelo tourist office if you want directions or more information, or even a map of the local public transport network if you want to return to your van by motorized transport!

Overnight spot

41°33'10.3"N | 8°22'51.8"W

Santuário do Bom Jesus do Monte

Some of you may have made the trip to Portugal with just one objective: to take the oldest funicular in the world that still uses water as a counterweight. Okay, we wouldn't bet on that, to be honest. For everyone else, it will be a bonus!

So here's a spot that will fulfil your spiritual, geographical and cultural needs. Flat, shady, with a toilet and located at the foot of the 577-odd steps leading up to the Santuário do Bom Jesus do Monte (but which you can dodge thanks to the said *elevador* for €1.50 one way or €2.50 return), this free car park offers quick access to this unusual site, as well as the option of hopping onto a bus to Braga city centre just a few stops away (takes 30 minutes and costs €1.65). Perfect, you said?

The northern parks

Viana do Castelo

Our dalliance with the Atlantic coast of Portuguese is coming to an end. We drove along it, more often at some distance from the shore than up close during the last days of our ascent to the north-western corner of the country, and Viana do Castelo was where we said goodbye before heading back inland.

The Spanish border in the north will now guide us for the final kilometres of our journey, taking us back to within a stone's throw of the entry point for our adventure in Portugal, two months ago.

For this last section, the northern region still has some lovely settings in store for us in scenery that we are already imagining will be sumptuous, with the Peneda-Gerês and Montesinho parks in particular as highlights on the programme. Not to mention other discoveries such as the carnival traditions of the Bragança region or the vinho verde of the Alvarinho. So let's go full circle and complete the loop in style!

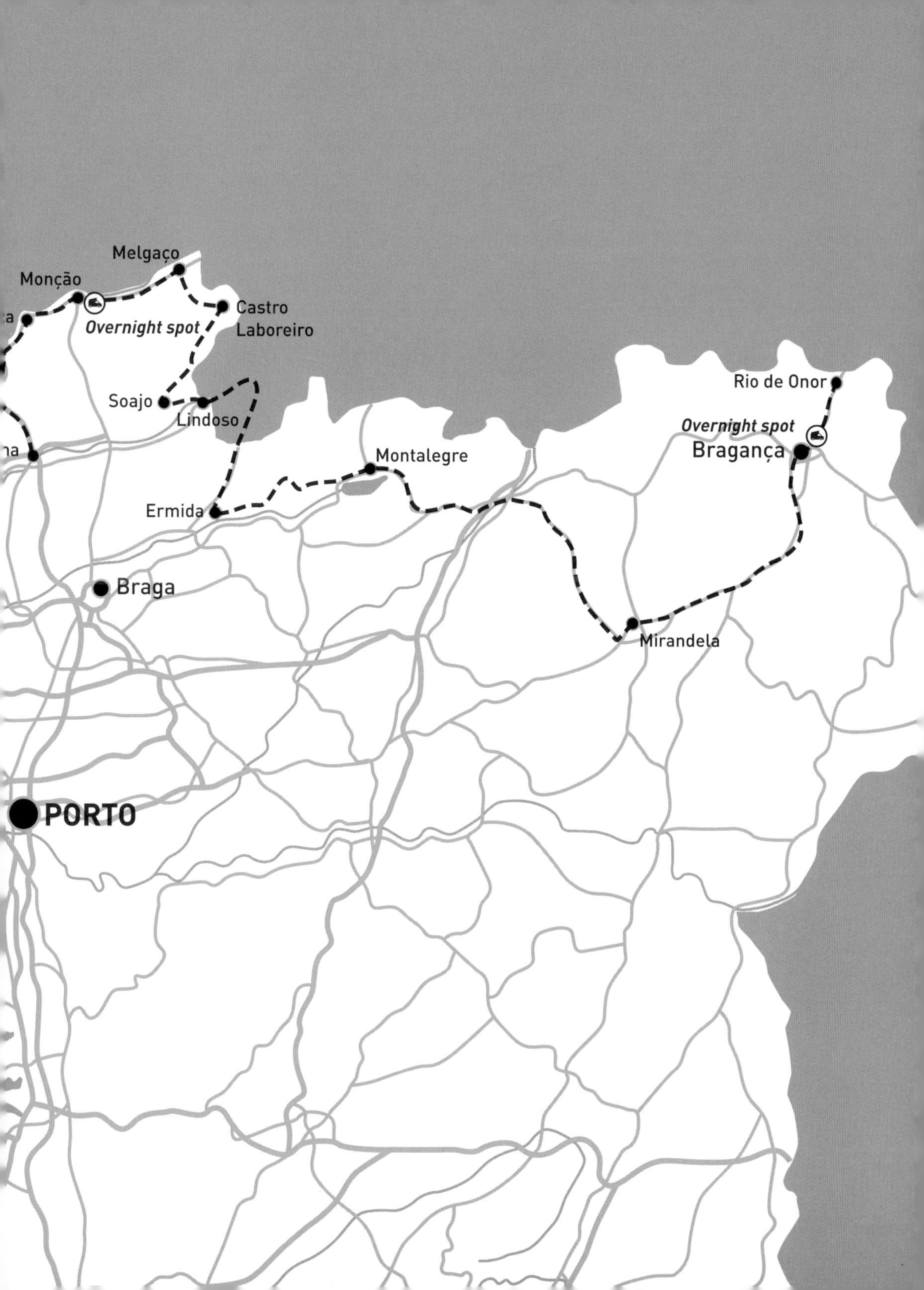
Melgaço
Monção
Castro
Laboreiro
Overnight spot
Soajo
Lindoso
Rio de Onor
Overnight spot
Bragança
Montalegre
Ermida
Braga
Mirandela
PORTO

A Monday at the market

Ponte de Lima 'Lima Bridge', as we're sure you'll be able to work out by now. A town with a devastating historical charm, taking its name (as you may have guessed) from the old medieval bridge that made the town famous, itself the successor to an older structure built by the Romans in 1 CE. The Portuguese road to Santiago de Compostela passes over this bridge.

What makes us park the van in downtown Ponte de Lima, though, is not so much the architecture as the need to find a post office to pay our motorway tolls. Once that's been dealt with, we take advantage of one of the rare spells of clear weather at the end of November to visit this pretty town. Which is how we end up in the middle of the famous market.
There's a real buzz on the south bank of the Lima! Every other Monday, dozens of stands and stalls are put up along the riverside. You can find clothing, flowers and accessories but above all stalls of fruit and vegetables, cheeses and delicatessen items or pastries and other local products – all of which will let you refuel before setting off on new adventures.

Finally, if you are in the area between May and October, take the day off to go and enjoy the International Garden Festival. This is an exhibition in which architects and landscape designers from various countries compete creatively with installations designed to fit a theme, which changes every year. The entrance fee is one euro per person (free for children under 12); check the opening times as they vary from month to month. More information from www.festivaldejardins.cm-pontedelima.pt/

♫ Glasgow Love Theme - Craig Armstrong

The 'green wines' of the North

Ponte de Lima marks our arrival in northern Portugal, a region that may not enjoy the international allure of the Upper Douro or the Porto area but is also well-known for its wine-growing. Those who were not lucky enough to arrive in Ponte de Lima on a Monday can to go to the Centro de Interpretação e Promoção do Vinho Verde to get some information or even for to taste the said vinho verde, the oenological specialty of the region.
But as we were lucky enough to see the market and you can't have everything, there was no CIPVV for us. So we launched ourselves (at a legal speed of course) along the Alvarinho wine route, featuring wines produced exclusively by around fifty estates grouped around the municipalities of Monção and Melgaço. Our route first takes us to the Miradouro do Monte do Faro, near Valença. A place with parking flat enough to spend the night, plenty of picnic tables, a restaurant, and above all a beautiful view of the surrounding area as far as Spain, which isn't far away.

A few minutes later we were welcomed at Quinta das Pereirinhas by the owner himself, Carlos Pereira. It's a far cry from the colossal dimensions of Porto's port cellars or even the producers of the Upper Douro. With 14 hectares and a production of around 100,000 bottles a year, Carlos Pereira does not pretend to compete in terms of quantity.

On the other hand, the dedication to his vineyard and the family-run business (4 employees, including himself, his wife and one of his sons) have made Quinta das Pereirinhas a must in the small world of Alvarinho wines. In fact, one of its flagship vintages has been given a quality award three years in a row by the

Comissão de Viticultura da Região dos Vinhos Verdes (CVRVV). The Concurso da Região dos Vinhos Verdes, known in short as Os Melhores Verdes, is very important because its 'Best of' award determines the five wines each year that will represent the Vinho Verde region abroad. So thanks to his Quinta das Pereirinhas Superior wine, Carlos has been one of the 'green wine' ambassadors to the world!

This former policeman's passion for his wines is tangible in their production, which is carried out from start to finish behind the house. Its young, fresh and very mineral wines will delight both connoisseurs and the curious for an average price of 7 euros a bottle (available all year round at the *quinta*).
Don't miss a conversation with Carlos (luckily for us, he speaks French!) over a glass of vinho verde, in his garden or his small museum-cum-boutique. He will be happy to show you his operation, from the vinification vats to the still where he also produces a brandy (for his personal consumption), to the bottling machine or the barbecue where he cooks the sheep he raises himself (again, always for personal consumption!). We bet you'll leave with a bottle, a jar of wine jelly or a bottle of olive oil!

A little further on, in Melgaço, we venture to Solar do Alvarinho, the information centre set up by the municipality in an impressive building that was formerly used as a courthouse. Further investigations give us a better understanding of the specific nature of the Alvarinho. It owes its fresh, mineral characteristics on the one hand to the region's soil, rich in granite and schist, and on the other to the microclimate enjoyed by the area: wet and cold in winter, very hot and dry in summer but with nights that remain cool. This contrast between diurnal and nocturnal conditions allows better maturation of the wine during the day while favouring a good preservation at night. Once again, don't hesitate to learn more about the region by treating yourself to a tasting or stopping by the shop selling local produce!

Quinta das Pereirinhas

Av. Prof. Doutor Pacheco de Amorim 725,
Vila Nova - Troviscoso, 4950-821 Monção

Overnight spot

42°04'46.4"N | 8°28'29.8"W

The hot springs of Monção

Spending a night at a car park in a town does not always mean settling for second best. So anyone who fancies treating themselves to an evening out in Monção can rest assured that there is an opportunity to spend a quiet night close to the centre that is as good as the prettiest overnight spots in the surrounding countryside.

The solution is the car park of the Monção thermal springs, located on the banks of the River Minho. Large, flat, with beautiful trees and public toilets (closed at night), it is just 300 metres from the town centre. The municipal swimming pool is close by, so there's even the possibility of taking a shower for just a few coins. Finally, the wooden footbridge beside the watercourse, the small thermal springs park, its picnic tables and the children's play area even let you spend a few pleasant moments during the day.

Heating system

A fridge that can be used as a freezer, a two-ring gas hob, a cruise control that also monitors the distance to the vehicle in front... As both a car and a camper van, the Marco Polo is packed with accessories at the cutting edge of comfort. Foremost among them is its fabulous heating system for when you're not on the move. Totally independent, this heater runs on fuel from the van when the engine is switched off. A safety system automatically stops it when a certain threshold is reached.

Even though it's not yet really cold in Portugal in November, a few minutes of warm air in the evening when raising the roof or in the morning when getting out from under the duvet are always welcome.
But we appreciate the stationary heating less for the heat it brings than for its ability to dry out the air inside the van. As the Portuguese coast can be humid, the highly effective blower really helps dry your towels, tea-towels and sheets!

On cold nights, those who suffer from the cold will also be happy to know that the Marco Polo's on-board computer allows the heating to be programmed to start and stop at whatever times you want.

Parque Nacional da Peneda-Gerês

We'll start by telling you right away that the Parque Nacional da Peneda-Gerês (PNPG) is undoubtedly the most beautiful park in Portugal, as well as being its only national park. Though that depends on individual taste, of course. But in our eyes, even at the end of November and even in the fog and clouds that partially mask the views, even under the torrential downpour through which we try to make our way along the winding roads, the beauty of the park is undeniable. At every turn, at every moment.

However, the particular charm of the PNPG is not only in its scenery. It is also unique for its biodiversity and above all for the way it is managed. All the animals in the park, whether domesticated (such as the native species of cows, sheep and horses) or wild (such as the half-dozen wolf packs, the deer fleeing the Spanish hunting zones, as hunting is forbidden in the park, or the Pyrenean ibex that was reintroduced here) can come and go in total freedom.

Its uniqueness is also manifest in the way of life of some of its inhabitants (around Castro Laboreiro), semi-nomads who relocate from one home village to another twice a year, for winter and for summer. They have also adopted a communal lifestyle in which various facilities are maintained and shared by all. In

particular, these include the ovens where the local bread (Pão Castrejo) is made – as dense and delicious as you could want. Workshops are offered by Montes de Laboreiro where you can take part in making the bread yourself! (www.montesdelaboreiro.pt/)

Last of all, it is difficult not to mention the setting of the park: its granite ridges that slice into the sky, the torrents that flow through it, the canyons that carve into it and the thick woods that cover it. Everything here reminds you of a movie set in a landscape forgotten by man, until you come across remains from Roman times or the ruins of medieval castles. Though anchored in the past, the Parque Nacional da Peneda-Gerês has also adapted to modern life. So you can learn more from the five mutually independent *portas* (each with its own website) that enclose the park's 72,000 hectares. These 'gates' are information centres where you'll find everything you need to make your visit a success. They have details of the activities available in the park (multiple hikes including a 296 km major hiking route, rafting, canyoning, mountain biking, horse riding, etc.) or information about the nature and history of the five cantons that manage the area (megalithic tombs, castles, fauna, flora, etc.).

There are also several campsites in the park; these are the only places where it is possible to spend the night. Stopping is even forbidden altogether along certain roads, even if only for a few minutes, but it's a price well worth paying to ensure the preservation of all aspects of this unique site!

A day in Peneda-Gerês

Whereas our first visit to the park yesterday was during heavy rain, our second day is greeted by a permanent drizzle, accentuated by an almost omnipresent fog. This adds a certain charm to the place to be sure, but the area is best visited during the months of May-June or September-October. There'll be no hiking or other outings for us, but nothing prevents us from enjoying the exceptional beauty of the park, while staying close to the roads. And to tell the truth, in this weather these roads become imbued with an almost mystical atmosphere that brings out the colours of autumn. Here is a sample of the places you mustn't miss in the PNPG.

Our itinerary starts at the Porta de Lamas de Mouro where we find out about the most interesting hiking trails in the north of the park. Ac-

cording to the person we spoke to, the Trilho Castrejo is one of the most attractive, a historically and culturally themed route of almost 17 km (about seven hours) that can also be shortened if you want. With a maximum altitude of 1,124 m, its intermediate level of difficulty gets you some magnificent views of the park. And as it's a loop, you'll find your van back where you left it when you get to the end!

From the gate, we take the N202 towards Baleiral, a magnificent route along a valley next to a mountain river that has been unleashed by rainwater. The turns keep coming, one after the other, until we discover a treasure whose presence seems incongruous, hidden in the middle of nowhere: the Santuário de Nossa Senhora da Peneda, built on the spot where the Virgin appeared to a shepherdess on 5 August 1220 (yup, a very precise date). The place is amazing, highlighted by the waterfall further up the mountain, overlooking the main building. A must-see, both close up and from afar!

We continue heading south, in particular via the M530 along which there are several natural pools, the first of which doesn't seems to have a name yet is very accessible thanks to a massive picnic area with easy parking (GPS coordinates 41°52'49.9"N 8°16'06.6"W). For another swimming spot, you can go to the Poço Negro! There aren't many roadside parking spaces but you can park in Soajo, 500 me-

tres away, and then walk or cycle there. And while you're in Soajo, take the chance to admire the famous *espigueiros* before going to Lindoso where there are even more of them! These outdoor granaries of wood and/or stone were once used for drying maize. They're closed at the ends and raised, a design that's all about keeping them free of rodents. As for protection against evil spirits, the crosses at either end were also watching over the grain!

If the weather is on your side and you have the time, one fairly easy hike is a loop starting from the town of Soajo, charmingly named the Caminhos do Pão e Caminhos da Fé, or in English 'the paths of bread and the paths of faith'. A journey that will take you back in time to the age when bread was synonymous with survival and baking it took on an almost spiritual dimension.
A little further south-east, we take a dog-leg via Spain to catch the awesome N308-1 from the north (the famous road in the middle of a forest that has remained untouched and where parking is forbidden) and savour its phantasmagorical atmosphere, before venturing into the heights on winding but no less incredible roads, notably the M1276! To find it, go down the N308-1 and – right in the middle of a bend – turn left towards Pedra Bela and the Arado waterfall, then just follow the tarmac (or your GPS) to Ermida and then Fafião. Pick up the N308 there, taking you to Montalegre.

We can now hardly keep count of the beautiful waterfalls, the superb viewing points, the copses where time seems to have stood still. We could provide you with an exhaustive list of the roads we went on and we'd definitely still be a long way from having toured the park fully. The best way would be to devote a healthy week to it so that you can take all the roads that cross it. And whenever your GPS gives you a choice, pick the route that stays within the PNPG park limits for longest.

Montalegre, a town stop

The Parque Nacional da Peneda-Gerês is now behind us and Montalegre appears on the horizon. Situated about ten kilometres to the east of the park exit, it is an ideal stopover for refuelling, thanks in particular to its Intermarché, which has not only a service station but also washing machines. Travellers who've spent a week hiking around Peneda-Gerês can wait for their washing machine cycle to complete and have a drink in the small cafeteria.

This "superb" hypermarket, although very practical, is obviously not the only point of interest in Montalegre. A castle dominates the historic city centre from the heights, flanked by an *ecomuseu* where you can learn a little more about the natural and historical heritage of the region. You can plan a visit to Pitões das Júnias, for example, one of the highest villages in Portugal, and its Mosteiro de Santa Maria das Júnias, an old ruined monastery dating back to the twelfth century.

Not far from the monastery, you will also find the Pitões das Júnias cascades, several spectacular waterfalls and basins that you can even cool off in during the summer. That means taking a walk of close on 600 m from the car park, a walk that includes a footbridge and a wooden bridge. A very fair price for such an absolutely amazing swimming spot.

Finally, a town stop wouldn't be complete without a convenient spot to bed down for the night and Montalegre is no exception to the rule. Various car parks are available both in the town and on its outskirts, but the Parque do Cávado wins the prize, as it is more pleasantly rustic than its counterparts (GPS coordinates 41°49'45.1"N | 7°47'17.2"W).

Great addresses we found

Pastelaria A Castrejinha

Ponta da Estrada,
4960-061 Castro Laboreiro

For some of the best bread you've ever tasted (and Clémence is the granddaughter of a baker!), the Pão Castrejo. It'll set you back about €3 per kilo.

Camper van travel and rainy days

When you organize your trip by van, you imagine yourself enjoying beautiful days on hiking trails, white sandy beaches, lovely sunny roads... You don't always allow for the rainy days!
As with all holidays, however, even if we choose to go during the best period, we are still subject to the same unpredictable factors. The biggest unknown being the weather.

So the question is what do you do if there's bad or terrible weather during a van trip?
• If you have the chance, take the opportunity to visit nearby museums, sights or monuments. It lets you stretch your legs and keep exploring and discovering things while staying dry!
• Find the nearest campsite and tick off the small chores that have accumulated: washing up, filling and emptying tanks, laundry, etc.
• Get cooking! It's been our new favourite rainy weather pastime since we got our oven for on the stove. There's nothing like cooking up a good meal to console yourself! Our winning combo: a big mug of tea or coffee plus a piece of cake and a good film or book! By the way, make sure you've got a laptop or tablet, a hard disk full of films and series or a subscription to a streaming site (preferably with the option of downloading content in advance) and/or books or an e-reader to save space. The van's accessory battery takes care of the rest!
• If you're miles away from everything, the storm is raging outside and the only option for you is to find something to do in 5 m^2, get out your duvet and have a nap or get out your cards and play! There's a wide variety of compact card and board games that are perfect for van travel! Some that we enjoy: Yahtzee, the Post-it game, Time's Up, Take 6!, Cards Against Humanity, The Werewolves of Miller's Hollow, Elixir and more.
• Get kitted out well enough to stick to the schedule regardless of the weather! Because you've ticked all the boxes on our checklist, you are of course prepared for any eventuality thanks to your all-weather gear (K-way jacket, rainwear trousers, etc.). So there's no reason why you can't go out and plough your way through a rainstorm (but don't take any risks). All the more so as the stationary heating will be there when you return to dry your things out and warm you up!

The faces of Bragança

♫ *Matilda - alt-J*

As we approach the final stage of our Lusitanian journey, the Montesinho Natural Park, we work on fine-tuning the preparations for the last visits so that we can finish in style! There's nothing better for that than calling on the tourist office, in this case in Bragança, one of the two municipalities responsible for managing the park (the eastern half is in Bragança and the western half is in Vinhais). With more than 30,000 inhabitants, the town also has all the amenities you may need for your road trip (supermarkets, service stations, etc.).

But that's not all! Lovers of history and Gothic architecture will enjoy a walk through the old town. The citadel and its castle, built between the eleventh and thirteenth centuries, are among the best preserved medieval sites in Portugal and are well worth taking in (the tour of the old town takes less than an hour). The view from the ramparts is fantastic too. And if you still haven't had enough, the dungeon now houses a military museum displaying weapons used by the Portuguese army from the twelfth century through to the twentieth.

Even that's not all! The Iberian Museum of Masks and Costumes is also on the itinerary for this visit, still inside the citadel walls. The Bragança region is also renowned for its carnival traditions! The festival season, a tradition going back more than two thousand years, lasts throughout the winter, with every town and village organizing its own carnival on a specific date. Something that no traveller criss-crossing Portugal between December and March should miss.

And that's still not all! Bragança also lays claim to gastronomic prowess, without you even needing to leave the old town. The excellent restaurant *Taberna do Javali* has some delicious dishes based on local products, including *javali* (wild boar) and Bísaro pigs raised in total freedom in the Trás-os-Montes mountains, where they feed mainly on chestnuts from the woods. Allow for about 25 euros per person at the restaurant. If you prefer an aperitif and snacks in the van, you can go to the municipal market to stock up on local produce, including traditional cheeses and smoked meats from the region (*fumeiros*).

Great addresses we found

Taberna do Javali

R. Dom Fernão 48, 5300-025 Bragança

Inside the citadel itself, the 'Boar Tavern' will delight you with typical dishes concocted from the products and specialities of the Trás-os-Montes region.
A full meal – tasty and plentiful – will cost about €20 per person. A huge favourite!

The municipal market

41°48'26.2"N | 6°45'49.6"W

Covered market, agricultural and authentic. Open every day. For stocking up on local products from Trás-os-Montes (boar, cheese, Bísaro pork, chestnuts, etc.).

Museu Ibérico da Máscara e do Traje

R. Dom Fernão 42, 5300-252 Bragança

For discovering the local carnival traditions and immersing yourself in them. Open every day except Monday.

Overnight spot

41°48'12.9"N | 6°44'47.1"W

The citadel of Bragança

At the edge of the town, at the foot of the citadel, Bragança's authorities have graciously provided a camper van park. Quiet, relatively flat, with public toilets (access from the road below, closed at night) and a wastewater collection point.

The terraced car park faces the Montesinho hills on one side and the old town ramparts on the other, so you can get to the castle district in under two minutes.

A tour of Onor

The sun is out for our last day in Portugal, albeit shyly. Starting from Bragança, we organized our schedule so that we would leave Lusitanian territory via the small village of Rio de Onor, which certainly has its oddities. An atypical place, just right for completing the huge loop of this adventure.

All the more so as it is situated on the edge of the Montesinho Natural Park, one of the largest in the country at an area of 75,000 hectares and the last compulsory stop on any good road trip in the north of Portugal. Bordered by Spain, the park has a setting that is bursting with charm and poetry in the autumn light. Its undulating plateaus overwhelm us with their beauty, punctuated by a myriad of sweet chestnut trees, whose bounty is one of the specialities of the region (Trás-os-Montes).

♫ *If You Leave Me Now - Chicago*

Of course, a nature park means activities. And if criss-crossing these routes isn't already enough of a journey in itself, hikers can also enjoy the Serra de Montesinho to the north of Bragança and the Serra da Coroa to the north of Vinhais. In particular, you can do a walk around Guadramil (start at the village, difficulty level intermediate to easy, 8.8 km loop) for a chance to spot some Iberian deer or wolves. (Don't forget your binoculars!) Starting from Montesinho, you can alternatively get to the eponymous summit via another 7.8 km loop (difficulty level intermediate to easy, with a climb of less than 300 m) and enjoy awesome views of the park. You'll find all this information and lots more at the tourist offices in Vinhais and Bragança, which manage the western and eastern halves of the park respectively. Be aware, though, that the region isn't nicknamed the Terra Fria for nothing: it is usually snowy during the winter!

What matters for us is that our crossing finally leads us to the Rio de Onor, known in particular for the way its community worked (until the 1990s anyway), an approach inherited from the Middle Ages. Until twenty years ago or so, the residents still shared their resources, worked together in the fields, used their own system of justice (fines paid in wine!) pronounced upon by a council made up of the heads of each family, shared the one and only breeding bull in the village, and so forth. All this information can be obtained from Ana at the Casa do Touro, the historic home of the famed bull. It has been turned into a small museum (free entry, open all year round on Wednesdays to Sundays from 14:00 to 18:00).

Nowadays, only the bar (open even in winter) still operates on the same basis, with four families running it throughout the year until Midsummer's Day, when they are replaced by others after the festivities (organized thanks to the profits generated by the bar). The village, built entirely of wood and schist stone, is magnificent and perfectly maintained, so it's well worth a stroll around. A campsite at the entrance of the village is available (in summer only) for adventurers who want to stay in the area.

No overnight stay at Rio de Onor for us, though. It's time to hit the road home and head back to France. We leave Portugal with more than a touch of sadness and already fully intending to return and explore the richness of this country in greater depth – its diversity, its almond blossoms and above all the generosity of its inhabitants. So it's not so much goodbye as "until we meet again"!

FJ-095-GE

2 months of Portugal for Fernão and us!

In figures, it's:

63 days for the total journey

8,600 km of which nearly 6,000 km were in Portugal

13 petrol stops (about 1,200 euros for 800 litres)

30 *miradouros*, at the very least!

39 *pastéis de nata*, or thereabouts!

12 overnight stays at campsites (€177.50, which makes an average of €14.80 per night)

24 encounters with unusual people

3 days with a video maker

2 *shaper* workshop visits

2 nights in a hotel

15 restaurants

8 wine tastings (in 4 different regions)

1 olive oil tasting

2 boat trips (Tavira and Sagres)

4 hiking trails

1 anchor cemetery

12 of Portugal's 13 nature parks (we missed Alvão)

1 national park, the one and only!

1 westernmost point of continental Europe (Cabo da Roca)

1 highest point of continental Portugal (1993 m in the heart of the Serra da Estrela)

Innumerable beaches and surfing spots

A dozen memorable sunsets

1 sunrise while stand-up paddling

1 sunset while stand-up paddling

7 stand-up paddling falls (all for Thomas!)

1 ocean initiative with the Surfrider Foundation

10 kilos or so of litter collected from the beaches

24 empadas de frango, between us!

2 rivers descended by kayak (Douro and Mondego)

1 swim in water at 8 degrees (Portagem)

5 typical local recipes cooked in the van

A healthy fifty dolphins (Sagres)

7 puppies in the Serra da Estrela

1 visit to the vet

1 attack by a wild horse that was a bit touchy

1 seriously muddy occasion, the last day there!

Vanlife index

Acknowledgements

The *Drive Your Adventure* books follow one another and no two are alike! This second book was an intense epic, made easier by the support of some and made rich and unforgettable thanks to the moments spent with others. We would therefore like to thank:
Antoine for his know-how and serenity when we ourselves had doubts about our work.
François for his watchful eye, always sharp yet constructive.
Adrien, a worthy representative of La 5ème Étape, who had to accommodate our choices. Thanks for your hard work!
Caroline, Stéphane and all our friends at Mercedes. A trip by camper van is the best!
Bertrand from Park4Night, for a tough but very well conducted launch interview!
Nel for being extremely cute, even if she's sometimes a bit annoying too.
All the people we met on the road, for giving their time and making this trip such an incredible adventure: Pedro, Antonio and Nina, Sílvia and Delfina, José and Tiago, Suzette, Rebecca and Nuno, Flo and his camera, Nelia, the Herdade do Esporão and Luis, Vera, Natura Algarve, Holly and David, Ana and Sara, Beatriz, Bruno and Miguel, Rui, Nico, Mélanie, Lisa, Afonso, Gonçalo, João, Daniel and Pedro, Flo and Pistachio, Eurico, Jonas and Gonçalo, the large Symington 'family', João and Tiago, Claudia and Manuel, Carlos and many others.

And finally our families, who continue to support us and take care of the Lieutenant in our absence.

Clémence, Thomas and Nel

Index of towns and villages in chronological order

Along the Douro

At the heart of the country

Heading south

Around Lisbon

La Costa da Prata

Porto the Grand

The northern parks